What
AN

"Burton Barr Jr. bares his soul... It is his hope that he will spare the reader of some of the heart ache he experienced. He writes in a warm conversational style that draws the reader into his life as he shares his story. Burton struggled with the results of his bad choices for over twenty years. Much like the parable of the prodigal son from Jesus' teaching, Burton remembered his (Heavenly) father's the call of God on his life. He once more responded to that call and has turned his life around. Instead of pursuing a drug abuse and drug dealing he is now leading a ministry reaching out to prisoners."

- Richard R Blake, The Midwest Book Review

"For those of you who need inspiration or just feel like you've gone too far for God to care, taking the time to read this book will let you know that it is never too late for God. Burton Barr Jr. has written an unbelievable testimony to the **Amazing Grace** of God and his unconditional love for us, which is something we all need to be reminded of at times."

- Books2Mention Magazine

"Burton Barr Jr. lets us know God can see good in us and we can be saved from ourselves. Barr does all this without being preachy or overbearing. It is a very good book and so very uplifting. I enjoyed every word..."

- Alice Holman, The RAWSISTAZ Reviewers

"Burton Barr Jr. writes a personal true testimony of his struggles with drugs and alcohol. I was surprised at how brutally honest Mr. Barr is, he held back nothing when writing this book. He was a true drug addict who stole from his jobs and family to fuel his habits. He was in and out of prison countless times until he finally put his trust in God. Only then was he able to succeed in being the best husband, father and most importantly the best man he could be. From what I read in this book it is only by the grace of God that Burton Barr is alive to tell his story today. His experiences are real. He is a living inspiration to all."

- LOCKSIE Arc Book Club

"Burton Barr Jr. unveils demons that he's battled consistently in his life span. As a son, husband, father, con artist, thief, inmate and junkie Burton has fallen many times. It just confirmed for me that we've all fallen and it's by the grace of God that we can get up. While reading as he ran the streets of Chicago, St. Louis and San Diego I wondered what would be the deciding factor for him to decide that God has already got a plan for him. See he'd already fallen, gotten back up, dusted himself off and attempted to do right, YET every single time there was always an obstacle just waiting for the chance to present itself. Isn't that life?"

- OOSA Online Book Club "O.O.S.A."

"I am honored to have been an inspiration to Reverend Burton Barr, who remains an inspiration to myself and the world around him. I feel blessed to have the gift of music by which to speak to the world of hope and change. Burton Barr's book is personal and honest. His story reveals God's infinite power to heal."

- Maya Azucena, National Recording Artists

"No matter what you have done or who you have become, God still loves you."

- Rev. Burton Barr Jr.

TO GREG & BESSIE BE BLESSED — *Burton Barr Jr.*

AMAZING GRACE

The Storm Is Passing Over

by BURTON BARR, JR.

KOBALT BOOKS

Kobalt Books LLC
Philadelphia

Cover Design by Rob Viper
Cover Model: Cedric Mixon
Book Edited by Cedric Mixon
Library of Congress Control Number: 2008929385

"Junkyard Jewel", by Maya Azucena
© 2007 Azucena Songs Music, LLC
"Children of the Night", by The Stylistics
© 1972 Alfred Publishing Co., Inc.
"I'm Popeye The Sailor Man", by Muel M Lerner
© 1933 Samuel M Lerner Publicaions/SONY ATV HARMONY
© 1873 Fanny J. Crosby, **"Blessed Assurance"**
"Amazing Grace", by John Newton
© 1779 Olney Hymns, Book 1, Hymn 57

For information:
Kobalt Books
P.O. Box 1062,
Bala Cynwyd, PA 19004
Printed in the U.S.A
www.kobaltbooks.com

Published by Kobalt Books L.L.C.
An original publication of Kobalt Books L.L.C.

This book is dedicated to the loving memory of
my dear, sweet cousin,
Juanita Jones

To two of my best friends
James "Cy" & Vernon Williams
who passed away while I was
writing my first book

To my long time friend
Paul Antwon Jones
who also passed away while I was
Writing this book

To the late Bishop Richard Burris
of Transformation Christian Church
In St. Louis, Missouri,

To two of my oldest friends
James "Gip" & Vivian Gipson

To my brother, Ralph &
my sister, Shirley

And to all of my family members
that means so much to me:
Christopher, Sharon, Dewayne,
Valisha, Tenesha, Tawana,
Darron, Maya, Terrell,
DeShawn, LaStarr,
& all of the others.

TABLE OF CONTENTS

Acknowledgments

I thank the Almighty God for allowing me to write this book. He has allowed me to go through many things during my life and He has never left me nor forsaken me.

I thank my lovely wife, Charlotte, for helping me put this book together and putting up with me when I was in my "leave me alone" moods.

I thank my friend and mentor in prison ministry, Rev. Jerry Hodges for all he has taught me. He really has a great compassion for the men and women who are incarcerated. He is truly a man of God.

I thank my niece, Christine Moore, for the inspiration that she has been to me. Even when I was at my worse she still saw the best in me. She never gave up on me and wouldn't let me give up on myself.

I thank my cousin, Rev. Patrice Jones for always being there for me with encouraging words and a prayerful heart.

I thank my friends, Michael "Brother Boogie" Anders and Nathaniel Johnson. Those brothers are truly dedicated to the work of prison ministry and aftercare.

I thank one of my newest friends, Maya Azucena for her inspiration and help in reaching the outcast of our society.

I thank my friend, Rev. Dr. Herman Toles, for teaching me how to write through sermons.

Although I acknowledged him in my first book, I want to thank my pastor and friend, Rev. Dr. Ronald L. Bobo, Sr. There is never enough that can be said about him and his lovely wife, Darlean. I truly love them both.

Finally, I want to thank my friends, Rev. Dr. Rosalind P. Denson who taught me the true meaning of integrity (and believe me, it was not an easy task), and Rev. Dr. Darlene Davis who has always been a great help to me and keeps me grounded.

INTRODUCTION

On a cool, cloudy evening in 1969, I sat alone in my apartment waiting for Tadpole to come by. It had become customary for us to get together each Friday after work and get high. We always met in my apartment because I lived alone, therefore, we didn't have to worry about our parents or siblings interfering with our fun.

Although my father had preached to me all of my life about the dangers of drugs, I really couldn't see any harm in smoking a little weed, popping a few pills, or snorting a few lines. Besides, I figured that since I was grown and living on my own, I should be able to live my own life and make my own decisions. So I sat there waiting for my friend.

When the doorbell finally rang, Tadpole was not alone. He had B.B. and Ronnie with him. Although I knew them, they were not guys that I normally hung out with. You see, my father had always warned me to stay away from "that crowd", but I let them in anyway.

As we filed into the dining room and started to gather around the table, I could sense that there was something wrong. Maybe it was the blank stares. On the other hand, it could have been the way they kept glancing at each other. Either way, I could tell that there was something that wasn't right.

I looked at my friend, desperately searching his eyes for some clue as to what was going on. Although I had known Tadpole almost all of my life, it was as though I was looking into the eyes of a stranger, and then it happened.

Silently standing in a state of shock as I watched Tadpole take a needle and other paraphernalia out of a paper bag. I was so dazed that I didn't notice B.B. and Ronnie circling around and coming up behind me until it was too late. As they were holding me down in one of the chairs and wrapping one of my neck ties around my arm, I couldn't believe what was happening. My friend, my very best friend was coming toward me with a needle and an eyedropper (a make shift syringe) filled with heroin.

I was only able to utter one word as I stared helplessly at Tadpole. "Why." He just looked at me and said, "I'm sorry, Bub, but I know that this is the only way that I can get you to try it." Tadpole stuck the needle in my arm and squeezed the bulb of the eyedropper releasing the heroin into my vein.

At first, all I could think about was revenge. However, when the drug began to spread through my system, a feeling of euphoria came over me.

After that night I lived the life of a drug addict. I eventually turned to a life of crime, trying to support my habit. I was in and out of trouble and in and out of jails and prisons all across the country. I was hurting everyone that loved me while blaming the ones that had started me on heroin years before, for the things that I was doing. I said, "It is not my fault. They are the ones that did this to me. It's their fault."

One Sunday morning my life took a turn for the worse. I had just purchased the drugs that I would need to get me through the first part of the day. By that time, I had become a "speed-baller," meaning I would mix heroin and cocaine together and shoot them both at the same time.

As I was walking home that morning with the drugs in my hand, I passed by a church and was able to hear the sermon that was being preached. There was something about that sermon that got my attention. It was the story of the prodigal son, also known as, The Lost Son. (Luke 15: 11-32)

I already knew the story. I had preached it many times myself. You see, I had been a preacher before I walked away from God and His church. Now I was a dope fiend that was living in a world of hopelessness. Just like the young man in the story, I had left my Father's (God's) house for the fast life of "the far country."

During that time, I had been shot, stabbed, arrested more than 30 times, been to prison three times, and had overdosed on drugs more times than I can remember.

At first, I just slowed down so that I could hear some of the sermon. Before I knew it, I found myself sitting on the church steps, crying like a baby and saying, "Lord, I am sorry. I am so sorry. Please forgive me for the life that I have been living. I am so sorry."

Although I didn't deserve it, God saved my soul and delivered me from a life that was full of misery and pain. I know that the only reason that I am alive today is because of God's love, and His Amazing Grace.

CHAPTER ONE

Don't Hate the Player, Hate the Game

In my first book, entitled The Hoodlum Preacher, I talked about a well-known pimp that operated on the West Side of Chicago. I met him one Saturday afternoon in a barbershop, called Freddy's. Freddy's was a place where many of the players got their hair done. It was the 1970's and most of the players were wearing "Super Fly" perms.

For the benefit of those who may not know what players are, they are the people who live the fast life. They are the people who live on the edge. They are the pimps, the hustlers, the con artists, the gamblers, and so forth. They are called players because they play games on people that are designed to separate them from their money and their possessions.

While sitting in the chair, he talked about the flamboyant lifestyle of players. He said, "You know, there are two kinds of people in this world, the players and the squares. The squares have to get up and go to work everyday because that's the only way they can make any money. They don't know how to play the game. They're too busy living their dull, boring lives and trying to stay out of trouble, but us players, we know the game. We drive the baddest rides. We've got the prettiest women. We've got all the money, and we do whatever we want to do, whenever we want to do it." Then he said, "I don't know about y'all, but as long as I live, I'm gonna be a player."

That was how I lived my life for the next eleven years, before I went back to prison. I was in the state penitentiary in Joliet, Illinois. I had been sent there for violating my parole when I was busted with a dime bag of cocaine.

One day I was sitting on the floor, chained and shackled to some other prisoners when I heard a voice that sounded somewhat familiar. Although I couldn't see who was talking, he said something that sounded even more familiar.

He said, "You know, there are two kinds of people in this world, the players and the squares. The squares are at home with their families, right now. They're eating what they want to eat, going where they want to go, doing what they want to do, whenever they want to do it, but us players, we're sitting here on this cold, hard floor, all chained up like a bunch of animals. We've got somebody telling us what to do, where to go, what to eat, when to eat, and when to sleep."

Then he said, "I don't know about y'all, but whenever I get out of here, I'm gonna be a square. Cause I ain't got to live like this."

Because of our rebellion and disobedience, we sometimes put ourselves in difficult situations. The Bible is full of stories about men and women who were called or chosen by God, but for one reason or another they strayed away from Him and everything they had ever been taught. Unfortunately, many of our jails, prisons, and cemeteries are full of them too.

I remember walking down 115th Street in Chicago one Sunday evening in 1984. I was trying to hustle some cop-money to buy some heroin and cocaine. It was during the Christmas season and many of the houses were beautifully decorated. As I walked along, I could see some of the people in their homes as they were decorating their trees. Some of them were sitting around, laughing and talking while enjoying themselves with their family and friends. I could tell that some of them had just gotten home from church.

My mind went back to the years before I had started drugging. I thought about all of the fun that I used to have with my family and friends. I thought about the Sunday mornings that I had spent in church with my brother, my grandmother and my Aunt Ruth. I thought about the night that I preached my first sermon when I was 17 years old.

I thought about all of the good jobs that I'd had and how people in my church and community had looked up to me. I thought about how proud my parents and family had been of me.

Now, all of that was over. I was no longer that up-and-coming businessman in the retail industry. I was no longer that young dynamic preacher that everyone was talking about. Now, I was that junkie who would con his own mother out of her last dollar so I could fill my veins with the poison that I needed.

How had I gotten to this point? How had I messed my life up so badly? I just wanted to be one of the players that were out there hustling and trying to make my mark in the game of the streets.

When I walked down that street that night I saw something that really scared me. I saw myself. That's why I will never forget the night that I walked down 115th Street. That was the night that I realized that I was just another dope fiend. That was the night that I realized that I was just another player, walking the streets in search of a victim. That was the night that I realized that I was just another lost soul living in a world of hopelessness.

Hopelessness: We see it everywhere. We see it in our homes. We see it in our schools. We see it on our jobs, in our streets and in our communities.

Hopelessness: We see it in the faces of the children who don't have enough food to eat, and we see it in the attitudes of our young people who are part of a school system that doesn't care if they receive an education or not.

Hopelessness: We see it in the tears of that mother who is struggling and doing the best she can to raise her children all by herself, and we see it in the heartache of that grandmother who has to raise her grandchildren because their mother is strung out on drugs.

Hopelessness: We see it in the despair of that man, who cannot find a decent job, and we see it in the disappointment of the ex-convict who is trying his best to do what is right but no one is willing to give him a chance.

Hopelessness: We see it in the pain of that child whose father is in prison, and we see it in the souls of the prisoners who are being warehoused rather than being rehabilitated. **Hopelessness**.

I spend a lot of time ministering to people all across the country. In doing so, I have seen so many men and women, both young and not so young, who are lost and hurting. They are tired of the way that they are living. They are tired of drinking. They are tired of drugging. They are tired of prostituting. They are tired of jailing. They are tired of playing the game. They want to climb up out of the pigpens of degradation and despair but they just don't know how.

They think that they have no hope because they are sinners and God hates them, but God does not hate sinners. He sent His Son to die for them. What God hates is sin. Sin is the game that Satan tricks us into playing. So don't hate the player. Hate the game.

CHAPTER TWO

Superman Don't Wear No Coat

When I was a child, my favorite television program was Superman. I would race home from school everyday and plop down on the couch next to my grandfather just in time to hear the announcer's opening words. "Faster than a speeding bullet. More powerful than a locomotive. Able to leap tall buildings in a single bound."

Then the scene would shift to one of the street corners in Metropolis, and all of a sudden, you would hear somebody say, "Look. Up in the sky. It's a bird." Someone else would say, "It's a plane." Finally someone else would shout, "It's Superman." Then you would see Superman flying across the sky with his cape flapping in the wind.

After the program was over, I would go into my bedroom and pretend to be Superman. I had a t-shirt that I had drawn a big "S" on with a red crayon. I would put it on and tie one of my mother's bath towels around my neck and try to fly across my bed. Although I was just a child, I wasn't crazy enough to jump out of the window and try to fly across the street. We lived on the second floor. Even if I had been successful in flying across the street I still would have been in trouble because I wasn't allowed to cross the street by myself. So I restricted my flying to my bedroom.

There were so many people that were caught up in the Superman frenzy; they came out with super everything, Superboy, Supergirl and Superdog. They even came out with a mouse that was flying around and beating up all of the cats in the neighborhood. They call him Mighty Mouse.

I loved Superman. He was my hero. I loved to see him beat up the bad guys and crush their guns with his bare hands. I loved to see him crash through concrete walls, but most of all, I loved the way that he stood for "Truth, Justice and the American way".

One day, during the Halloween season, my mother took my brother, Ralph, and me to Sears to pick out our costumes. When I saw the Superman costumes I didn't have to look any further. I knew exactly what I wanted. I was going to be Superman.

I didn't need that t-shirt with the "S" drawn on it anymore. I had a real "S" for my chest. I didn't need the bath towels anymore, because I had a real cape. Although Halloween was almost two weeks away, every evening I would put on my costume and become

Superman. I couldn't wait until Halloween came so I could finally wear my costume outside for everyone to see.

However, when the big day had finally arrived, the weather had turned cold, but I didn't care. I put on my costume and headed for the door. My mother stopped me and said, "Wait a minute, boy. Go in there and put your coat on." I looked at her and said, "Superman don't wear no coat." She said, "I said go in there and put your coat on". I said, "But Superman don't wear no coat."

Mother gave me one of those looks, and then she said, "Either you put your coat on or you keep your tail in the house." I went to my bedroom and started mumbling to myself. "Superman don't wear no coat. Superman don't wear no coat." Then I put my coat on and went outside.

Apparently I wasn't the only one whose parents insisted that their children wear a coat, but that didn't make me feel any better, because no one could see the "S" on my chest or the cape on my back. Therefore, no one could tell that I was Superman. I just looked like everybody else. I just looked like another little kid with a coat on, but everybody knows that Superman don't wear no coat.

Some people think of Christians as super humans and the church as a place where the perfect people meet. That is why some people think that they are not good enough to go to church. They will say, "As soon as I get myself together, I will go to church." They think they have to stop drinking, stop drugging, or stop running the streets first; but that makes about as much sense as a sick person saying, "As soon as I get myself well, I will go to the hospital." Jesus wants us to come to Him just as we are. Then He will change us into who and what He wants us to be.

In reality, the church is a hospital for sinners. None of us are perfect. None of us have "arrived". We all struggle with some things, but we strive toward perfection. That is why we come together as a church family to worship God and to encourage and strengthen one another.

One day, a little boy went to his father and said, "Dad. What is a Christian?" His father, being one of the leaders in the church, was proud to tell his son what a Christian is, but after he had finished giving his explanation, the boy looked puzzled. Then he looked at his father and said, "Dad. Have I ever seen one?"

Unfortunately, some of us don't always look and act like Christians after we leave the church house. When we get out into the mean, cold world, sometimes we put our coats on. We look like everybody else because we have our coats on. We talk like everybody else because we have our coats on. We act like everybody else because we have our coats on. Therefore, people cannot see the Christ in us because we have our coats on.

Bench members are not the only ones that put their coats on when they are not in church. There are some deacons, ushers, choir members and even preachers who have been known to put their coats on after the benediction as well. Some of them are well known televangelists, while others are unknown pastors of storefront churches.

Those of you who read "The Hoodlum Preacher", know that I left the ministry and the church when I was 20 years old. I was a dope fiend for most of twenty-two years, from 1969 to 1991, and an alcoholic until 1993. In 1994 I went back to church and back to preaching the Gospel, and I was doing quite well, for a while.

I moved to Greensboro, North Carolina to go into business with a friend of mine. One day, I attended a birthday party in his backyard and drank a glass of wine along with the other guest. There is nothing wrong with having a little glass of wine, is there? Maybe not for most people, but I had been an alcoholic for almost 25 years. That innocent little glass of wine woke something up in me. Before I knew it, I was in the kitchen with the wine bottle turned up. After that, it was like I had never quit drinking.

The business failed and I returned to St. Louis. When I got back, I became a "closet drinker." I was too ashamed to let anybody know that I had a problem and needed help. I had too much pride. After all, I was Rev. Barr. I was in charge of the substance abuse ministry. I couldn't let people know that I was drinking again. So, after church was over and I wanted to go to the liquor store, I would change my clothes so I didn't look like a preacher. In other words, I put my coat on.

Jesus said that we are the light of the world. However, we cannot light up this dark world if we have our coats on. It is very important for the church of God to remember that we all need help sometimes, and when we do, we can call on Him who is able to keep us from falling (Jude 24). Just remember, Superman don't wear no coat, and Christians shouldn't either.

CHAPTER THREE

Super Saints

As I stated earlier, my favorite television program as a child was Superman, but I've often wondered what it was about Superman that fascinated people so much. What was the one quality that set him apart from everyone else and made so many people fantasize about what it would be like to be Superman or Superwoman?

After giving it some thought, I've come to the conclusion that it was because he didn't need anyone. No matter what the situation was, he didn't need anyone to rescue him. He could save himself. He didn't need the police, the fire department or the paramedics. As a matter of fact, they needed him.

The desire of many people, both male and female, is to accomplish mighty feats and gain status academically, professionally and even spiritually. Moreover, they want everyone to know that they and they alone, are the reason for their success.

That would give them bragging rights. Oh yeah, we love to brag. We brag about everything. Am I right? We brag about our children. We brag about our accomplishments. We even brag about our position in life.

There is nothing wrong with being all that you can be, and there is nothing wrong with trying to be the best in your chosen field. There is, however, something wrong when you start believing that you are better than everybody else.

Unfortunately, it is not only the secular world that has this superiority complex. It has drifted onto our churches as well. There are too many Christians that look down on other Christians, and I'm not just talking about one denomination that thinks they are better than another denomination, or one church that thinks that they are better than another church. I'm talking about Christians that are in the same denomination, or sometimes even in the same church, that think that they are better than everybody else.

I call them Super Saints. They will condemn a young lady if her skirt is not as long as they think it should be. They will reprimand a young man because he has the audacity to go to church without wearing a tie. However, the problem with Super Saints is that they are often times more successful at driving people away from the church, than they are at bringing them into the church.

Super Saints are not anything new. There were Super Saints in Jesus' day as well. One day, Jesus told a story about the Pharisee and the Tax Collector.

"To some who were confident in their own righteousness and looked down on everybody else, Jesus told this parable: "Two men went up to the temple to pray, one a Pharisee and the other a tax collector. The Pharisee stood up and prayed about himself: 'God, I thank you that I am not like other men – robbers, evildoers, adulterers, or even like this tax collector. I fast twice a week and give a tenth of all I get.'

But the tax collector stood at a distance. He would not even look up to Heaven, but beat his breast and said, 'God, have mercy on me, a sinner.'

I tell you that this man, rather than the other, went home justified before God. For everyone who exalts himself will be humbled, and he who humbles himself will be exalted."(Luke18: 9-14 NIV)

Just who were the Pharisees, anyway? I'm glad you asked. They were the Super Saints of that era, but you don't have to take my word for it. Just look at the prayer that he prayed. He did not start by thanking God for His goodness and mercy. He started by thanking God that he was not like everybody else. In other words, he was better than everybody else, and then he started bragging about how good and how righteous he was, and what he did and did not do.

The Super Saints of today are the same way. They love to stand in the churches and brag about how holy and how righteous they are. Then, just like their role model, the Pharisee, they start patting themselves on the back and bragging about how glad they are that they are not like Brother Bob or Sister Sue. They keep running from church to church, in search of the one church that is as holy as they are. They think they are going to Heaven because they deserve to be there. They don't know anything about God's grace. The only grace they are familiar with is their "Aunt Grace."

I told you earlier that I was a big fan of Superman when I was a child, but I have discovered that Superman and Super Saints have a lot of things in common. I just want to point out a few of them.

First of all, the only thing that we know about Superman's past in that he came from the planet known as Krypton, but we don't know anything about his lifestyle while he was there. Did he have super powers there too, or was he like everyone else?

And just how did he get to be Superman anyway? It seems like he wants everybody to believe that he was born that way. He has always been Superman. He has never been like everybody else.

That is the same way that some of the Super Saints are. You never hear them talk about what God has delivered them from because they want everybody to believe that they have been saved (Christians) all of their lives. They have never been sinners and they have never done anything wrong. If you let them tell it, they were born holy. As a matter of fact, when they were born, and the doctor slapped them on their behinds, they didn't even cry. They just said, "Praise the Lord, Saints. Praise the Lord."

When God delivers you from something, He gives you a testimony, and your testimony can help somebody that is going through some of the same things that you went through.

Another thing we know about Superman is he has a secret identity. He is not Superman when he gets to work. While he is at the Daily Planet he becomes an entirely different person. He becomes mild mannered Clark Kent, because he doesn't want anybody there to know that he is Superman. In other words, he puts his coat on.

Therefore, while he is at work, he doesn't look like Superman. He doesn't dress like Superman. He doesn't talk like Superman. He doesn't act like Superman. He doesn't do the things that Superman would do. As a result, no one at his job knows that he is Superman. Although Lois Lane might have her suspicions, the closer she watches him the more convinced she becomes that he is not Superman, because she saw him do some things or heard him say some things that Superman would not do or say.

It is the same with some of the Super Saints. They also have a secret identity. No one on their job or at their school knows that they are Christians. They just want to fit in and be part of the crowd. They want everybody to like them. They want street credibility.

Therefore, while they are there, they don't look like Christians. They don't dress like Christians. They don't talk like Christians. They don't act like Christians. They don't do the things that a Christian would do.

There might be someone that works with them or goes to school with them who knows that they go to church. However, after they watch them for a while, they'll say, "He is not a Christian" or "There's nothing to her" because they saw them do some things or heard them say some things that a Christian would not do or say.

Another thing we know about Superman is that he has X-ray vision, meaning he can see through things. In other words, Superman can see things that no one else can see.

Super Saints have X-ray vision too. They can see everything that is wrong with everyone else, but for some reason they can never see anything that is wrong with themselves. They will condemn a drug addict for breaking into somebody's house and stealing their television set, and then turns right around and buys that same television set from that same drug addict if the price is right.

Through the years, Superman has caused the death or injury of a lot of children who were trying to be like their hero. Many of them jumped off rooftops or out of windows trying to fly, only to go crashing to the ground.

Likewise, Super Saints have caused the spiritual death, or at the very least, caused some Christians to backslide because they intimidated them with their "Holier than thou" attitudes. As a result, they ended up chasing them away from God and away from the church.

On the other hand, there are people who are in church every Sunday who are still struggling with drugs, alcohol, gambling problems, or sexual sins. They are miserable but they are afraid to seek help from anyone because of the Super Saints. So they suffer in silence, hoping no one will ever find out.

If you are wondering how I know so much about the Super Saints; it's because I used to be one of them. I wanted people to think that I was so holy and perfect, but I discovered that I wasn't fooling anyone but myself. So I went from being a Super Saint, to being a Super Sinner.

However, I thank God for introducing me to someone. His name is Mercy. So when I get weak and stumble along the way I can fall down on my knees and call on him.

That's why the songwriter said:

Your grace and mercy brought me through
I'm living this moment because of you
I want to thank you
and praise you, too
Your grace and mercy brought me through
Justice demanded
that I should die
But Grace & Mercy said "No, no.
We've already paid the price"
I once was blind
but now I see
Your grace and mercy rescued me

CHAPTER FOUR

The Wild Mouse

When we were children, my father used to take my little brother, Ralph, and me to an amusement park named, "Riverview." It was located on the North Side of Chicago. We really enjoyed all of the games and the rides that we went on, but there was one ride that I would never get on. It was a huge roller coaster was named, The Bobs.

There was always a long line of people that were waiting to get on The Bobs, but for the life of me, I couldn't understand why. That was the biggest, scariest looking thing that I had ever seen. People would be yelling, screaming and crying while they were riding on it, but after the ride was over, those crazy people would get back in line so they could ride on that thing again.

Some of my friends tried to talk me into riding on The Bobs. They called me chicken and scare-de-cat, but I didn't care. There was no way that I was going to get on anything that went that high off of the ground. Period. Ralph and I rode on the safe, sensible rides like The Merry-Go-Round or The Ferris Wheel. One day, we found a ride that we had never been on before. It was called, The Wild Mouse. It had the same kind of seating that The Bobs had but it just rolled around the park on level ground and into a tunnel. There was a long line there too, but it looked like it was a nice, safe ride.

Ralph and I got on The Wild Mouse and took the seat that was in the front. We rode along, waving to people until we entered the tunnel. The farther we got into the tunnel the darker things became. We couldn't see anything, not even each other. Although the tunnel was a little scary, it was fun. The train moved along very slowly, almost like The Tunnel of Love. We were laughing and talking and enjoying the ride.

Finally, after the long ride through the tunnel, we saw daylight ahead. We thought we were coming to the end of the ride, but when we came out of the tunnel we found out that we were no longer on the ground. When I looked down I couldn't even see the ground. I think I saw The Bobs down there. I looked ahead and it looked like the tracks were coming to an end. I looked at Ralph and said, "Uh oh."

Remember, Ralph and I was on the front row. I wanted to cry, but before I could get anything out we were flying down that long, steep track at about a million miles an hour. Everyone was screaming, "Awwwwwww", but I was yelling, "Daddaaaaaaay"

I had never been so glad to get off of anything in my life. All 12 years of it. I had no idea that the ride that seemed so nice and peaceful was a roller coaster in disguise. I didn't know that while we were enjoying that long, slow, uneventful ride through that long, dark tunnel that we were getting further and further off of the ground until it was too late. However, what surprised me was, as scary as The Wild Mouse was, a lot of the people got back in line to ride it all over again.

You might not know it, but Satan has a Wild Mouse too. It is called sin. We all have ridden on it at one time or another during our lifetime. Millions of people are still riding on it today. The Wild Mouse. Some of its riders are easy to recognize. They are drug dealers, drug addicts, alcoholics, Gang bangers, prostitutes, rapists, robbers, players and player haters just to name a few. However, there are a lot of respectable citizens that are taking the ride as well. The sad thing is they don't even realize it.

All of their lives they have avoided the crazy, dangerous roller coasters like The Bobs. In other words, they stayed out of trouble, received a good education and they are pursuing the American dream. Some of them are doctors, lawyers, bankers, teachers, politicians, community leaders and hard working family people. They think they are traveling on nice, safe level ground as they cruise through, what they think is, the tunnel of love. However, when they reach the end of the tunnel they will realize that they are riding on The Wild Mouse and they are just as far from level ground as the people that are riding on The Bobs.

When I got off of The Wild Mouse that day I knew that I was never, ever going to ride that thing again. I didn't like the ride, but there were others that loved the thrill and excitement, so they rode that thing over and over and over again. For the life of me, I just could not understand how they could do that. It is the same way in life. Some people accept Christ and walk away from the world of sin and ungodliness, but there are others that continue on that path because they love the thrill and excitement of it, or it could be that they just don't know any better. However, it doesn't matter whether you are riding on The Bobs, The Wild Mouse, or walking on level ground (living a Christian life) you are still a long way from perfection. We all are. *As it is written, there is none righteous, no, not one. (Romans 3:10)* Although none of us will ever be sinless, by the grace of God we will sin less each day that we live.

CHAPTER FIVE

Trapped In a Closet

I attended a grammar school that was on the West Side of Chicago, named Lawson. It was located on the corner of 13th Street and Homan Avenue. In those days we stayed in the same classroom all day long, sitting in alphabetical order while the same teacher taught all of the subjects.

My 5th grade teacher was Mr. Sanchez. I will never forget him because he picked me up by my ears one day when he saw me grab one of my classmate's breasts when we were returning from recess.

Another thing I remember about Mr. Sanchez's room was I sat in the third seat in the first row. The reason I remember that so well is because a girl named Mae sat in the seat in front of mine. Mae was a short, mean, light skinned, ugly little girl that resembled a ten year old, female Mike Tyson. She was a little bully and everyone in our class was afraid of her, including most of the boys.

In those days there were a lot of neighborhood gangs. Mae's older brother was the leader of one of the most notorious gangs of that time. Therefore, nobody messed with Mae. I mean NOBODY.

One day, Mae decided that I was going to be her boyfriend. She didn't ask me about it either. She just told me that that was how it was going to be. If that wasn't bad enough, she told me that the next day I was going to kiss her.

I did not want to kiss Mae, but I didn't want to get beat up either. So when the next day came around, I didn't go to school. I told my mother I was sick. Well, it was somewhat true, because the thought of kissing Mae upset my stomach, but that only worked for one day. So after that, I did the only thing that I could think of. I played hooky everyday.

My mother and father both worked, so there was no one home during the day. Therefore, I stayed home and watched television all day. Although I had started playing hooky because I didn't want to face Mae and her brother's gang, it had gotten to be fun. I started ditching school everyday. The only problem was my grandparents lived downstairs on the first floor, so I had to be very quiet so they couldn't hear me, but our floors squeaked in certain places and one day my grandfather heard me and came upstairs to see who was up there. When I heard him coming up the back stairs I ran into my bedroom and hid in the closet.

The closet that Ralph and I shared was not very neat. In fact, it was down right junky. We had more clothes piled up on the floor than we had hanging on the rod, but that worked in my favor that day.

When I heard Papa open the back door, I got all the way in the back of the closet and covered myself up with everything that I could get my hands on. I heard him as he walked around the house, looking in every room. When he walked into my room, it seemed like I could hear my heart pounding. I heard him grunt when he got down on his knees and looked under the bed. Then I heard the closet door open. I had never been so afraid in my life. I knew that Papa kept a gun in his house, and I was just hoping that he didn't start shooting. If he would have found me hiding in that closet, I would have been dead anyway, because my father would have killed me for playing hooky. Dad didn't play that.

I was relieved when I heard the closet door close and Papa walking out of the bedroom, but my joy was short lived. Instead of him going out the door and back down stairs, he sat down in the kitchen and started talking on the phone. Since the kitchen was right next to my bedroom, I had to stay in the closet.

After that, Papa started coming upstairs everyday and hanging out. Maybe he just wanted to get away from my grandmother for a while, but everyday I had to run and hide in the closet. At first, hiding in the closet was fun; it was like a game to me, but after a while that game became old, and playing it was not much fun anymore. I had gotten tired of that closet. It was hot in there and I couldn't watch TV anymore or get anything to eat. I couldn't even go to the bathroom. Ditching school was not much fun anymore either, because day after day I was trapped in a closet.

I decided it was time to go back to school and face Mae. I didn't know what was going to happen when I got there. Really, I didn't care. I was just tired of being trapped in that dog-gone closet.

Day after day we see hundreds, or perhaps thousands, of men and women that are trapped in one closet or another. Some of them are trapped in a closet of alcoholism. Some of them are trapped in a closet of drug addiction. Some of them are trapped in a closet of sexual immorality. Some of them are trapped in a closet of gang violence. Some of them are trapped in a closet of hopelessness.

This world is full of various kinds of closets. There are closets of racism, homosexuality, prostitution, hatred, pride, jealousy and gluttony just to name a few. We enter into some of our closets voluntarily. Others we rather wander into unconsciously. Some of our closets are large while others are quite small. Some of them are neat while others are filthy.

Sometimes we go into the closet to get away from something or someone. For a while, our closet experiences might be fun. We enjoy the carefree lifestyle and the excitement of living on the edge. Besides, when you are hiding in a closet, people cannot see the real you. However, sooner or later your closet is going to become uncomfortable. In other words, you are going to start feeling some of the consequences of the decisions that you have made.

I have been trapped in a lot of closets during my lifetime. We all have. The Bible says, "There is none righteous, no not one." We have all messed up and made mistakes, but people like to categorize sin. In other words, my sin is not as big or as bad as your sin.

For years, my friends and I shot cocaine in our arms. Ralph and his friends used to look down on us because of that. However, at the same time, he and his friends were freebasing or smoking crack. It was still cocaine. During the same time, there was another group of people that looked down at all of us because we were either shooting cocaine or smoking cocaine, but they were snorting it. Whether you are shooting it, smoking it or snorting it, cocaine is still cocaine.

The point that I am trying to make is, to God, there is no big sin or little sin. Sin is sin, and although He loves the sinner, He hates the sin, all of it.

It doesn't matter what you have done or what you have become, God loves you. So come on out of that closet. You don't have to be trapped any longer. Jesus has opened the door for you and He is standing there with His arms wide open, saying, *"Come unto me, all ye that labor and are heavy laden, and I will give you rest. Take my yoke upon you and learn of me; for I am meek and lowly in heart; and ye shall find rest in your souls."* (Matthew 11:28-29)

CHAPTER SIX

A Message from Hell

When I was in prison, a Christian newspaper was circulated each month. There were a lot of nice articles in it along with some very interesting testimonies about inmates and former inmates that had accepted Jesus Christ as their Lord and Savior and had turned their lives around.

What I remember most about that paper was a poem that I saw in it. The title was, *"A Message from Hell."* I read that poem over and over again, but it would be years before the words that were recorded there would take on a very special meaning to me. In fact, it took the death of one of my oldest and dearest friends for me to understand what the "Message" was saying. Before I tell you the words of this poem, allow me to tell you a little bit about my friend, Fuzzy.

I was about 14 years old when Gip and some other friends of mine introduced me to a new kid that had just moved into the neighborhood. He said, "Hey Bub, this is Fuzzy." I looked at Fuzzy and I said, **"Fuzzy Wuzzy was a bear. Fuzzy Wuzzy lost his hair. Then Fuzzy Wuzzy wasn't Fuzzy was he?"**

Everybody started laughing, except Fuzzy. He started chasing me down Christiana Avenue. I was laughing the entire time that he was chasing me. By the time he caught up with me, he was laughing too. We have been friends ever since.

Fuzzy lived on Roosevelt Road and Christiana Avenue above a tavern that was named, "The Heat Wave." He lived there with his father, grandmother and his brother, Billy. He was about a year older than I was and very streetwise. His grandmother used their apartment as a gambling establishment and she also sold bootleg liquor after hours.

I was somewhat jealous of Fuzzy and the way he lived. He had complete freedom to come and go as he pleased and to do whatever he wanted. He didn't go to school, he always had plenty of money, he was a sharp dresser and the girls were crazy about him. He was kind of like "The Fonz" on Happy Days.

Fuzzy and I had been through a lot together during our teenage years. We played together, fought together, and were almost killed together. Yeah, Fuzzy was one of my best friends.

We lost contact for a few years, when I was called into the ministry in 1965 and later moved to Cleveland, and then to Detroit. I eventually moved back to Chicago, but I backslid, leaving the ministry and the church. When that happened, Fuzzy was one of the first people that I ran into. We picked up right where we had left off, but by then we were both smoking marijuana.

As time went by, I started snorting and shooting heroin and cocaine. I convinced some of my friends to do the same. Fuzzy was one of them. In fact, I was the one that first stuck a needle into his arm.

Fuzzy and I got high together quite often. Eventually, I renewed my relationship with Jesus Christ and was delivered from my drug addiction. Nevertheless, I never told Fuzzy or any of my old friends about my deliverance. I kept putting it off, waiting for a more convenient opportunity. Unfortunately, it never came.

One day I received a phone call from my mother telling me that Fuzzy was dead. As bad as that news was, what Ralph told me hurt even more.

Whenever someone starts dealing heroin in a new neighborhood, they sometimes give away sample packets to potential customers in an effort to win their business. That's what happened on Christiana one day, but that time, the heroin was laced with arsenic. Everyone that shot or snorted some of it died. That was someone's way of getting rid of some junkies. Fuzzy was one of them. His grandmother found him on the floor in his bedroom with the needle still in his arm.

When I heard that, I was devastated. My best friend was gone. I kept thinking that if I had only had the chance to talk to him and tell him about how God had delivered me from drugs, my friend would still be alive. Then I realized that I had had more than one chance but I kept putting it off. Now it was too late. My friend was gone.

When I got home that night, I walked into my bedroom and sat down without even turning on a light. As I sat there, my mind went back to the poem that I had read years ago while I was in prison. I seemed to visualize a dark, gloomy figure walking towards me with a piece of paper in his hand. He said, "I am a messenger from the damned. This is a letter that I was asked to deliver to you. It is from a friend of yours who is in Hell now. It says:

Dear Friend,
I stand in judgment now, and feel that you are the blame somehow

While on earth, we walked day by day, but never did you lead the way
You knew the Lord in truth and glory, but never did you tell the story
My knowledge then was very dim. You could have led me safe to Him
We were together here on earth, but you never told me of your second birth
Now I stand this day condemned, because you failed to mention Him
You taught me many things, that's true. I called you friend and I trusted you
Now I know, but it's too late. But you could have kept me from this fate
We walked by day and talked by night, and yet you showed me not the light
You watched me live, and let me die, and you knew I'd never live on high
Yes, I called you friend in life. I trusted you in joy and strife
And yet in coming to this end, I see you really WERE NOT my friend.

Fuzzy

I don't know if Fuzzy is in Hell or not. Only God knows that, but what I do know is that I saw my friend headed down the path of death and destruction and I did absolutely nothing about it.

Unfortunately, too many Christians are guilty of that very thing, and millions of people are suffering because of it. We have all been delivered from something. None of us were born holy, but we sit in church Sunday after Sunday, hiding behind our sanctified walls and stained glass windows while singing, "Send me, I'll Go" and then we go to our favorite buffet after the benediction and do nothing. We cannot make anyone change the direction that they are going, but we can let them know that there is a better way, and Jesus is that way.

I have that poem and a copy of Fuzzy's obituary on the wall in my office. Hardly a day goes by that I don't see his face. It serves as a reminder for me to tell somebody about Jesus that day.

Sometimes I get tired of seeing Fuzzy's face, but there are so many other faces that I am even more tired of seeing. I'm tired of seeing the faces of teenagers who are behind prison walls and will be there for the rest of their lives. I'm tired of seeing the faces of grieving parents and grandparents whose children are riding in the back of a hearse instead of riding in the back of a school bus. I'm tired of seeing the faces of all of those men and women who stand aimlessly and idly on street corners everyday looking for their next drink or their next fix.

Many of them feel like they are living in a world of hopelessness. They think the church is a social club for perfect people or they have done too much wrong for God to forgive them, but we must help them understand that no one is perfect. *There is none righteous, no, not one. (Romans 3:10)*

CHAPTER SEVEN

Bobo, Boogie and Bub

I was introduced to church and Christianity at a young age. My parents sent Ralph and me to Sunday school every Sunday, but that is not unusual. Many people, especially us baby boomers were in church.

Unfortunately, as I grew older I strayed away and wandered off in the wrong direction. That is not unusual either, but some of us stray further away than others, and for some of us, the road back is long and painful.

I want to tell you a little bit about some of the people that I know that have traveled down the road that I am talking about. They are some of the strongest Christians and community leaders in the country. You might look at them now and think they have never committed a sin in their entire lives, but the Bible says, **"All have sinned, and come short of the glory of God. (Romans 3:23)**

The first person that I want to tell you about is my pastor, Reverend Doctor Ronald L. Bobo, Sr. He is truly a man of God. He is not only my pastor; he is also my prayer partner and friend, who actually wrote the foreword for my first book.

Pastor Bobo is a man of character and integrity. He stands up for what is right, no matter what the consequences are. He has a hunger for lost souls and compassion for those who are hurting. I have learned a lot about how a Christian man is supposed to act by observing him. I have seen how he treats his wife, how he provides for his family and his unwillingness to compromise his conviction for the sake of fame, fortune, or friendship.

Pastor Bobo has preached and taught the word of God on almost every continent of the world and he has led thousands of men and women to Christ. I have seen God use him mightily, time and time again, but he is the first one to let people know that he too has made some bad choices during his life. Although he grew up in a strong Christian home and accepted Christ as his Savior when he was a child, I have heard him preach many times about how he stumbled while he was away at college.

Although Pastor Bobo did not travel down the road to death and destruction for the length of time that some of us have, the point I am trying to make is no one is without sin. *"If we say that we have not sinned, we make Him a liar, and His word is not in us." (1 John 1:10)*

The next person I want to tell you about is Michael Anders, better known as, "Brother Boogie." Brother Boogie is one of the most loyal and dedicated ministers to ex-offenders that I have ever known. He is truly about God's business when it comes to loving and caring for the men and women that society has blown off. He will spend his last dime trying to feed and find housing for people when they are released from prison.

I believe Brother Boogie loves God more than he loves himself. If people didn't know better, they would think that Brother Boogie has been a Christian all of his life, but the truth is that he met Jesus while he was in prison for bank robbery. That was how he supported his gambling addiction. As a matter of fact, he robbed the bank where his wife worked. That almost destroyed his family, but that's how Satan operates. His mission is to steal, kill and destroy.

Although Satan intended to harm Brother Boogie by causing him to go to prison, just as in the case of Joseph, *"God intended it for good to accomplish what is now being done, the saving of many lives." (Genesis 50:20b)*

Before I tell you about Bub, I want to take a minute and tell you about a couple of other brothers that are on the battlefield for the Lord. One of them is Nathaniel Johnson.

Nathaniel is the head of one of the most successful aftercare ministries in the St. Louis area. That brother is so strong in the Lord; you can almost feel the presence of God hovering over him when he talks, and he loves to talk about Nehemiah rebuilding the wall of Jerusalem and comparing it to modern day Christians rebuilding relationships with the community at large.

Nathaniel reminds me of another Biblical personality, the Apostle Paul. Before Paul met Jesus Christ he terrorized a lot of people with his brutality. Before he gave his life to Christ, Nathaniel was one of the most notorious gangsters in the St. Louis area. I think he spent almost half of his life in prison, but now he uses that same tenacity and zeal in an effort to bring men and women to Christ.

The other person that I want to tell you about is my hero and mentor, Reverend Jerry Hodges. I first met Rev. Hodges when I was an inmate at the Cook County Jail in Chicago. He was there, faithfully, every Sunday evening, preaching and teaching the word of God. At that time, I thought I had done too much wrong for God to forgive me. Does that sound familiar? Rev. Hodges told me something that I have never forgotten. He said, "It doesn't matter what you have done or what you have become, God still loves you."

That is the message that I deliver to men and women who are in jails and prisons all across this country. It is the message of hope and of love. Rev. Hodges has been preaching that message and sharing the love of Jesus in jails and prisons for almost forty years. He has single-handedly changed the lives of more inmates than I can even imagine. As a matter of fact, it is because of him that I am not in prison today. God has a mighty call on his life, but Rev. Hodges wasn't a Christian all of his life either. One of the mothers of the church, Mother York reached out to him and changed his life while he was incarcerated.

Although the title of this chapter is *Bobo, Boogie and Bub*, I really don't have to tell you that much about me. In case you don't know, I am Bub, and I was quite the sleazebag before Jesus came into my life. I also refer to my former lifestyle throughout this book.

All I am trying to say is your life is not over with just because you've messed up or made some bad choices, but you don't have to take my word for it. The Bible is full of heroes that messed up at one time or another. Let me tell you about a few of them:

- Adam and Eve disobeyed God
- Noah got drunk
- Moses murdered someone
- David committed adultery
- Peter denied Jesus
- Paul was an accomplice to murder
- Rahab was a prostitute
- Mary Magdalene was possessed with seven demons

John Newton was a slave trader who sold more than 20,000 Africans into slavery. After he met Jesus Christ he wrote one of the most famous Gospel songs of all time, Amazing Grace.

Amazing grace, how sweet the sound
That saved a wretch like me
I once was lost, but now I'm found
Was blind, but now I see

For all have sinned, and come short of the glory of God.
(Romans 3:23).

CHAPTER EIGHT

The Prairie Chicken

My father and my Uncle Archie used to tell stories to me all of the time. Over the years I used many of them in sermons. As time went by, I heard other stories told by Pastor Bobo, Rev. C. L. Franklin, Bishop T. D. Jakes, Billy Graham and many other preachers during their sermons. It's hard to remember from whom I heard which stories, but one of my favorites is the story of the prairie chicken.

One day, two little boys were playing in the woods when they happened upon two nests. One of them was an eagle's nest, the other one belonged to a prairie chicken. Both nests contained several eggs.

The little boys, being mischievous, took one of the eggs from the eagle's nest and put it in the nest of the prairie chicken. After the eggs hatched, the little eagle grew up with the prairie chickens, thinking he was one of them. He did everything that the prairie chickens did. He walked likes the prairie chickens. He clucked like the prairie chickens. He scratched around in the dirt searching for food just like the prairie chickens.

One day, the eagle was roaming around in the yard when something caught his attention. He saw a big, beautiful bird gliding effortlessly through the sky. He was mesmerized by the majestic creature. He turned to one of prairie chickens and asked, "What kind of bird is that flying up there?" "That's an eagle, the king of birds" replied his neighbor. "I wish I could be like him" said the eagle.

When the prairie chickens heard that, they all started laughing and teasing the little eagle. Then one of them said, "Quit wasting your time on foolish dreams. All you are ever going to be is a prairie chicken, just like the rest of us." After many years, the eagle died, still thinking he was a prairie chicken.

Satan has fooled a lot of God's children into thinking they are prairie chickens. Many of them grew up in the church. Some of them were ushers. Some of them sang in the choir. Some of them were even preachers or deacons, but somewhere along the way they ended up in the wrong nest. They ended up in a nest full of prairie chickens. Now they are doing everything that the prairie chickens are doing. They are walking like the prairie chickens. They are talking like the prairie chickens. They are thinking like the prairie chickens. They are digging in the dirt just like the prairie chickens.

In other words, they are going where the prairie chickens go. They are drinking what the prairie chickens drink. They are smoking what the prairie chickens smoke. They are shooting what the prairie chickens shoot. Some of them are even locked up in cages just like the prairie chickens.

You might be one of the people that I am talking about. You might be wondering if there is something better for you. You might be at the lowest point of your life right now. You may have dreamed of soaring with eagles but you are still hanging out with the prairie chickens because one of them has told you that that is all you will ever be. So you lowered your expectations and gave up on your dreams. You have lost your focus and your self-esteem. You think that all you can ever be is what you are right now.

Well, I've got some good news for you. God did not create you to be a prairie chicken. He created you in His image and in His likeness. God is not just a king. He is the King of Kings, and the eagle is not just a bird. He is the king of birds. If you belong to God, that makes you a child of the King. You are not a prairie chicken. You're an eagle. So get up out of that dirt, dust yourself off and start flying like an eagle, but the only way that you can do that is by putting your life and your trust in the hands of God.

William R. White told a story that's origin is found in Jewish oral tradition. After making a few changes, I have told this story in churches and prisons all across this country. I find it only fitting to be included in this chapter.

When God had nearly finished the act of creation, an announcement was made that the only thing left was to create a creature that is capable of understanding and marveling in the greatness of God. "They will be called humans," God said. "They will not only be on earth, but they will be created in my image. They will have reason, intellect and understanding."

However, Truth approached the Almighty God, pleading with Him not to create humans. "Oh God," Truth said. "I ask you to refrain from calling into being a creature that is capable of lying. The last thing we need is to have a world full of deception and fraud."

Then Peace came forward to support Truth's cause. "Oh Lord," he said. "I beg you not to create creatures that will disturb the harmony of your creation. I fear that these humans will act with revenge and initiate war."

Then Justice stepped forward. He said, "Dear Lord, I must agree with Truth and Peace. I think you will be making a huge mistake by creating humans. Before long they will be robbing, stealing and killing each other. Then this beautiful world that you have created will be full of jails, prisons and cemeteries."

While they were pleading their case against the creation of man, the soft voice of Love asked to be heard. He said, "Dear God, I know that any being that is created in your likeness will have the capacity to perform great deeds. Filled with your Spirit they will comfort the sick, visit the lonely, and provide shelter for the homeless. They will even minister to the prisoners that Justice spoke of. Such a being could not help but bring glory to you, Oh Lord."

Although the Lord listened to the voices of Truth, Peace and Justice before He made His final decision, it was because of Love that human beings were created.

When God created man, He did not create a perfect being. That is, He did not create people that are incapable of sinning, but because of His love for us, He is willing to forgive us for our sins if we ask Him. *If we confess our sins, He is faithful and just to forgive us our sins, and cleanse us from all unrighteousness. (1 John 1:9)*

CHAPTER NINE

Don't Follow Me! I'm Lost

Everyone who knows me knows that there is only one section of St. Louis that I am afraid to go into. Just the thought of driving through that part of town, especially at night, terrifies me.

It is not the so-called ghetto that frightens me. I was born and raised in the ghetto. I am not afraid to go into gang territories. That is where a lot of our ministries are based. It is not the drug infested neighborhoods that are destroying too many of our communities that I am afraid of. I was part of that culture for almost half of my life. So I don't mind telling you that I am not afraid to venture into any of those areas. However, there is one section of St. Louis that no one can get me to go into alone, and that part of the city that I am speaking of is named, Forrest Park.

For the benefit of those of you who are not familiar with the St. Louis area, let me tell you a little bit about Forrest Park. First of all, Forrest Park does not frighten me because it is a dangerous place. On the contrary, it is one of the safest parks anywhere, and it is not the people that frequent the park that I am afraid of. There is not a classier group of people anywhere.

Forrest Park is not located in a run down, neglected part of town. It is in one of the most prestigious neighborhoods. It is the home of opera houses, museums, golf courses, picnic grounds and the St. Louis Zoo.

Therefore, you might be wondering and asking yourselves, "What's the problem? If Forrest Park is so nice, beautiful and safe, why is he so afraid to go in there?" Well, I'm glad you asked. The reason I am afraid to go into Forrest Park is because, every time I go in there I get lost and cannot find my way out.

When I first moved to St. Louis, I asked my cousin, Darron, how to get someplace. He told me that the quickest way was to take the shortcut through Forrest Park. As I was driving through the park I noticed that there were a lot of turns, curves, and roads in there. It seemed like every turn that I made was the wrong turn and every road that I took was the wrong road. I had gotten to the point that I didn't care what street I came out on. I just wanted to find a street, any street.

I started praying one of those, "I'm not going to do it anymore" prayers. I said, "Lord, if you will just get me out of this park

I promise that I will never set foot in here again." You know the kind of prayer that I am talking about, the "I'm not going to do it anymore" prayer. You might have prayed one or two of them yourself.

I'm talking about the time that you drank too much and you were as sick as a dog, then you called on God and said, "Lord, if you will just get me over this drunk, I promise I will never drink again." I'm talking about the time you were out partying and getting high, and you spent your rent money or couldn't pay your car note, then you started praying, "Lord, if you will just get me out of this mess, I promise I will never do that again." I'm talking about the time you were arrested and ended up in jail or prison. You started calling on God, saying, "Lord, if you get me out of here, I promise I will do what's right from now on."

I found myself following various cars, hoping that they would lead me out of that park, but it seemed like I was just getting in deeper and deeper. What surprised me the most was when I looked in my rearview mirror and saw someone who was following me. I pulled over and said, "Hey man, don't follow me. I'm lost."

Jesus talked a lot about the lost. That is who He was most concerned with, those who are lost. In Matthew 10, He talked about the lost sheep of the house of Israel. In Matthew 18, He said, "The Son of Man has come to save that which was lost", and in Luke 15, He told three parables, one about the lost sheep, one about the lost coin, and the third one has become one of the most popular sermons known to man, and that is the story of the lost son, better known as "The Prodigal Son."

In Luke 16:19-31, Jesus told the story of two men. One of them is a rich man, usually called Dives, which is Latin for rich. The other man is a beggar named Lazarus. Some theologians believe that this is not a parable that Jesus is telling, but it is a historical account because in no other parable did Jesus refer to any of the characters by name.

Let us compare the lifestyles of these two individuals. First of all, the Bible says that Dives dressed in purple and fine linen. Wearing purple was associated with kingship. He lived in luxury, enjoying himself by eating sumptuously, meaning he dined on exotic and costly dishes everyday.

In most Bible stories, when they mention a gate, they are usually talking about a gate to a city, but Dives was rich enough to have a gate to his house. This brings us to the second character in this story, Lazarus, because that was where he was laid each day, at the rich man's gate.

The Bible says that Lazarus was happy, just to eat the crumbs that fell from the rich man's table, literary meaning, what he threw away. You see, in Biblical days there were no napkins or paper towels. Therefore, the rich would use pieces of bread to wipe their hands and fingers, and then toss them out of the window for the dogs, and that is what Lazarus would eat.

Now the story takes a dramatic turn. The Bible says that Lazarus died and was carried by the angels to Abraham's bosom. The rich man also died but *"in hell he lifted up his eyes."(v23a)*

I used to wonder why Dives went to hell. Just what had he done that was so terrible? After all, he had not ordered Lazarus to be removed from his gate, he made no objections to his receiving the bread that was flung from his table, and he was never deliberately cruel to Lazarus. So why did he go to hell?

Well, the sin of Dives was he never noticed Lazarus. He accepted him as part of the landscape and simply thought it was perfectly natural and inevitable that Lazarus should lie in pain and hunger while he wallowed in luxury. So it was not what Dives did that landed him in hell, but what he did not do.

The sin of Dives was that he could look on the world's suffering and need, and feel no grief or pity in his heart. He looked at a fellow human being, hungry and in pain, and he did nothing about it. His was the punishment of the man who did nothing. Dives passed right by Lazarus everyday and he never really saw him.

Let me ask you something, my friend. Who do you see? When you are on your way to church on Sunday mornings all dressed up in your finest outfit, who do you see? After the benediction, when you are on your way home to a nice Sunday dinner, who do you see?

Our streets and communities are full of people who are lost and hurting. Do you see them? Our cities are inundated with men, women and children who are homeless and hungry. Do you see them? Or do you turn your head and look away as if they don't exist?

Dives made a desperate plea that everybody needs to hear. He said to Abraham, "Please send Lazarus to my father's house. I have five brothers there. He can talk to them so they won't come to this place of torment." In other words he was saying, "Tell them, don't follow me. I'm lost."

You might not know it, but there is someone who is sending you that same message. They are saying to you loud and clear "Don't follow me. I'm lost." The message could be coming from a prison cell, a hospital bed or from the cemetery. My question for you is do you hear them.

CHAPTER TEN

Why Don't You Quit?

I love Jazz. I love listening to the sweet sounds of gifted artists such as: Miles Davis, Stanley Turrentine, Grover Washington, Jr., George Benson, Herbie Mann, Hubert Laws, and Wes Montgomery just to name a few.

One of my favorite musicians is the legendary Gene "Jug" Ammons. The first time I'd ever heard of him was when I was in The Star Fire Lounge, located on Homan Avenue near Grenshaw Street in Chicago. The D.J. was playing a cut called, "Ca' Purange (Jungle Soul)." I had never heard anyone play the tenor sax like that. Some time later, I heard other records of his, including, "Angel Eyes" and "Canadian Sunset." I was an instant Gene Ammons fan.

Ammons had recently been released from prison after serving seven years of a 15 year sentence on a narcotics charge. Shortly after his release, he put out a new album titled, "The Boss Is Back." My favorite tune on the album was a cut named, "The Jungle Boss", but I will never forget the time I heard him play one of Eddie Harris' cuts titled, "Why Don't You Quit?" They both had studied music under Walt Dyett while attending DuSable High School on Chicago's South Side. Jug almost made that saxophone talk that night.

Like many jazz artists of the 50's and 60's, Ammons was believed to have been addicted to heroin. Even with all of his success in the music industry and his two stints in prison, he was still unable to kick his habit. This is purely speculation on my part, but some of his friends and relatives that meant well probably kept asking him, "Why don't you quit?" Well, speaking from experience, that is easier said than done.

I was addicted to one drug or another, mainly heroin, cocaine or crack, for more than twenty-two years. During that time there were so many people; friends, relatives and law enforcement, that kept asking me that same question, "Why don't you quit?" I was never so tired of hearing any one question in my life. I can only imagine how tired Ammons was of hearing it. That is probably why he was able to play that tune with so much feeling.

Since I have been clean, the number one question that I hear has gone from "Why don't you quit?" to "How did you quit?" People want to know how I overcame my drug addiction. After writing my first book, some people asked me if I was going to write a sequel, detailing step by step how to quit doing drugs. I wish it were that easy but, unfortunately, it is not.

Millions of people are addicted to something: drugs, alcohol, cigarettes, gambling, pornography, etc. To those who are on the outside looking in, the solution seems simple. Just say no, but to those who are caught up in their various habits, it is a different story.

There are a lot of people that were able to turn their lives around by using different methods, but I can only tell you what worked for me and for hundreds of other people that I know of. It was by the power of God through Jesus Christ.

The problem is, people want to put God in a box. They think He only works in certain ways. However, God works in many ways and through many people and programs, but that is not what we were taught in Sunday school. Therefore, we are always looking for the Damascus Road experience or the miraculous deliverance.

God has miraculously healed many people from sicknesses and deadly diseases through prayer or the laying on of hands. Others had to go to the hospital or undergo surgery. Likewise, He has delivered a lot of people from drugs and alcohol after they gave their lives to Him. However, others had to go to treatment centers and attend Alcoholics Anonymous or Narcotics Anonymous meetings.

The truth is God sometimes uses doctors, hospitals, treatment centers, 12 step programs, or the power of prayer to heal or deliver us from our situations. Sometimes He even uses prison.

I don't know why God does what He does or why He works the way He chooses. When you get to Heaven, you can ask Him yourself, but maybe He has already given us the answer. *"For My thoughts are not your thoughts, nor are your ways My ways," says the Lord. "For as the Heavens are higher than the earth, so are My ways higher than your ways, and My thoughts than your thoughts."* (Isaiah 55:8-9)

The story was told of a man that was trapped on his roof during a terrible flood. As the water rose dangerously high, a man came by in a row boat to rescue him, but the man refused to get in the boat. He said, "That's all right. God will save me." The water had risen even higher when someone in a helicopter came to his rescue. Once again, the man refused help, saying, "That's all right. God will save me."

The water eventually rose above the man's head and he drowned. When he arrived in Heaven he was angry with God for allowing him to drown. He said, "Lord, why didn't you rescue me from that roof?" God said, "I sent a helicopter and a boat." God works in many different ways.

My father always told me that there are three steps to doing anything. He said if you follow those simple steps, there is nothing that you cannot do. With the help of the Lord, I used those steps to overcome my years of addiction. I don't claim to be an expert when it comes to recovery. There are people that have studied this area extensively and are more qualified than I am to talk about the subject. However, this is what helped me, and I believe that people can overcome many of their addictions if they fully commit themselves to these three steps. Hear they are.

STEP ONE: _WANT TO DO IT._

Unbelievably, this is the most difficult step of them all. When you conquer this step, you are half way there. Most people don't want to stop using their drug of choice because they are still enjoying it. All of their friends are getting high. They cannot imagine how life would be without it. Drugs have become such an important part of who they are, they cannot see themselves going through life sober.

I say that because I didn't really want to quit. I thought I did, but the truth is, I was just tired of the consequences of my addiction. I was tired of going to jail. Boy was I tired. Besides that, I was hurting all of the people that loved me. I had betrayed them so many times they no longer trusted me. I was not welcome in many of their homes or even in some of their churches. As far as they were concerned, I was a leper, an outcast, a vagabond.

My arms looked so bad because of the tracks (needle marks), I had to wear long sleeve shirts or jackets all of the time, even during summer months. My veins were becoming so damaged it was getting harder and harder for me to get a hit (find a good, open vein to stick the needle in). I had run con games on so many people; no one wanted to be around me, including other junkies.

I had gone to treatment centers on several occasions, but I never really gave it my all. I had even gotten high while I was on my way to the treatment center. Most of the time, I was just trying to appease someone or get out of the trouble that I was in.

I had thrown that needle and syringe off my back porch and into the alley over and over again, only to go crawling around on my hands and knees in the dark with a Bic cigarette lighter trying to find it. I had ripped off my father, my mother and my aunt so many times they couldn't even afford to buy food. I hated myself for what I had become and what I was doing to so many people, but I still could not quit.

When I was in prison, I had a recurring dream. I would have a syringe filled with heroin and cocaine. I would wrap a tie around my arm, but just before I stuck the needle in my vein, I would wake up. I was angry because I always woke up just when I got to the "good part."

Eventually, I made a vow to God and to myself that when I got out I would never stick another needle in my arm again. After spending almost a year behind bars and attending church regularly, I thought I had beaten the drugs. I was finally clean. However, the night before I was released, the cravings were back stronger than ever.

Although I had gone many months without drugs while I was in prison, in the back of my mind I wanted to get high just one more time. I had not completely surrendered my heart and soul to God. Consequently, I started shooting up again shortly after I got out. It was almost as though I had never quit using. My habit was worse than ever. I was completely out of control.

When an unclean spirit goes out of a man, he goes through dry places, seeking rest, and finds none. Then he says, "I will return to my house from which I came." And when he comes, he finds it empty, swept, and put in order. Then he goes and takes with him seven other spirits more wicked than himself, and they enter and dwell there: and the last state of the man is worse than the first. (Matt. 12:43-45 NKJV).

I had gotten to the point that I realized that if I continued living that kind of life I would soon be dead or in some very serious trouble. I had to become brutally honest with myself and stopped trying to run games on everybody, including myself, and accept God's help, **His** way. I had to make up in my mind, and determine for myself that I was ready to quit. In other words, I had to <u>want</u> to quit. Then, and only then, was I ready for step two. Are you ready?

STEP TWO: <u>*TRY TO DO IT.*</u>

This is a difficult step as well because it takes some effort. That effort is not limited to just saying no, going to church or attending support group meetings. It takes tenacity. It takes that same tenacity, commitment and persistence to get off drugs that it took to get a hold of your drug of choice.

I used to lay awake all night, scheming and dreaming of ways to get the drugs that I needed. There was no shame in my game. I did whatever it took. As far as I was concerned, going to jail was just an occupational hazard.

That is the attitude that you have to have when it comes to step two. If you are not willing to do whatever it takes to overcome your addiction, you are not really trying. You can't be ashamed to ask, or even beg, for help. You can't be afraid to go through the pains of withdrawal. How much pain are you going through now?

You might have to go into long-term treatment. If one center cannot accept you, find one that will. Don't take "No" for an answer. This is your life. You might have to stay away from some of your friends or relatives. Not everyone will want to see you succeed.

You cannot be afraid of failure. If one thing doesn't work for you, try something else. People will give up on you. The important thing is, don't give up on yourself, and don't stop trying. Don't stop trying. Don't stop trying.

My father once told me something that I will never forget. He said, "Son, if you slip and fall down in the mud, don't just lay there and wallow in it. Get up, clean yourself off and keep on going. If you fall down again, get up again. If you fall down again, get up again. If you keep falling down, keep getting up." **Don't stop trying**.

One Sunday morning in November of 1991, I was walking past a church after I had copped a one and one (a bag of heroin and a bag of cocaine). Somehow I was able to hear the sermon that was being preached. It was the story of the prodigal son. I had heard, and even preached that sermon many times before I'd walked away from God and the church, but that time it was different. I saw myself as the prodigal who had left home and God as the loving father who was waiting for my return.

I sat on the steps of that church, crying like a baby, and begging God to forgive me. I decided right then and there that I had to quit, but what would be different this time? How would I succeed this time after failing so many times before, and what would I have to do to increase my chances of success? It didn't take very long for me to figure it out.

I had to make some drastic changes in my life. Asking God to deliver me from drugs was one thing, but there were some things that I had to do for myself. First of all, I had to stop hanging out with my old crowd. How could I expect to stop using drugs if I was constantly surrounding myself with other junkies and dealers? I had to surround myself with positive people. I mean, people who were trying to make something of themselves. Not the players, hustlers and cons that I hung out with. The problem was I didn't know any. At least not any that wanted to have anything to do with me. So I decided to leave Chicago.

I moved to St. Louis. I knew many people that were in the drug game there, but I stayed away from them. It wasn't easy, but I was determined to make it that time. I kept getting penny-annie jobs. Every time they found out about my background, I was fired, but I refused to give up. I kept getting other jobs until finally I found one that didn't care about my past. With the help of my mother and some of my other relatives like Nita, Patrice and Christine I was able to make it. Although their love and support was a vital part of my success, it was my faith in God that brought me through. Although I slipped along the way, He did not let me fall.

It might take a while for you to complete the first two steps. Remember, there are no shortcuts. However long it takes, you must complete them before you proceed to the third and final step.

STEP THREE: _DO IT._

When you reach this step, you will find that you are free from the bondage of drugs. Now you will have to become free from the affects of your years of bondage.

When the Children of Israel were in slavery in Egypt, they prayed to God for deliverance. Eventually, God delivered them from their bondage. However, whenever things got a little rough, they wanted to abandon their journey to the Promised Land and go back to what they knew best. They wanted to go back to Egypt.

When things get rough, times get tough and disappointment comes your way, how are you going to deal with it? Will you return to the bondage of Egypt and medicate yourself with you drug of choice, or will you march on to the Promised Land? The time will come when you will say to yourself, "What's the use?" You might even think that you can get high just one more time. That is when you will have to remember that your sobriety is not a sprint. It is a marathon.

Whatever you have to do to remain drug free, do it. If you have to leave your family, do it. If you have to leave your friends, do it. If you have to move to another city, do it. Whatever you have to do, do it. Your life depends on it. So do it.

One day, Oprah did a show called, "Why don't they quit?" It was a very interesting and informative look at drug addiction and the inability of addicts to kick their habits. Part of the program was very technical, dealing with different parts of the brain and how it functions. I never knew that the brain was so complex. I was absent on the day that they taught about it in school.

That discussion made some people realize that quitting is not always that easy. I don't know if we will ever come up with an answer that we can all agree upon, but there is one thing that I am convinced of. As long as there are drug addicts, there will always be someone who will look down on them and say, "Why don't you quit?"

CHAPTER ELEVEN

Who Let The Dogs Out?

When we were children, Ralph and I had a dog, named Rex. Rex was a mean old dog. At one time or another, I think he had bitten everyone he had ever come into contact with, including my brother and me. He even bit my grandmother one day, and she was almost 70 years old. I think my father was about the only one that Rex didn't mess with.

The building that we lived in was a two family flat. My grandparents lived on the first floor along with my father's brother, Uncle Bill, and we lived on the second floor. Since it was a family building, the porches on the back were connected and fenced in. That was where Rex lived.

Everyone in our neighborhood knew who Rex was. Although he hadn't been off of the back porch very often, everyone that had ever walked through the alley behind our house had seen him, or at least heard him barking and growling while he was trying to get at them.

Ralph and I were not allowed to walk Rex. Our parents were afraid that if he got out, we would not be able to control him. I was hard headed, though. So one day I decided to take Rex for a walk anyway. I snuck and got his leash while my father was taking a nap and my mother was down the street at Mrs. Brown's house. I was going to show them that they didn't know what they were talking about. I could control Rex. He was a good dog. So I put the leash on him and we snuck out the back door.

I was doing just fine while we were in the alley and there was no one else around, but then we went through the gangway and came out onto Christiana Avenue. When Rex saw all of those people and they saw him all hell broke lose, and Rex did too.

That was a sight to see. People were running, screaming and jumping on top of cars. Some people were even trying to climb into first floor windows in an effort to get away from that crazy dog. There I was, running around, trying to catch Rex and get him back in the house before my parents found out what I had done. Just when I thought it couldn't get any worse, I saw my mother coming down the street yelling, "Who let that dog out? Who let that dog out?" I knew I was in trouble then.

If that wasn't bad enough, I saw my father coming down the stairs, but when he got outside, he didn't start chasing Rex or trying to catch him. He just stood there on the porch and said, "Rex. Come here." Just like that, it was all over. Rex just went over and sat down at my father's feet. After that day, Rex never got out of the house again, and for a long time, I didn't either.

We often bring problems on ourselves due to our disobedience. The sad thing is, many times we are not the only ones that are affected. Paul tells us that it was because of the disobedience of one man that sin entered into the world. You might already know the story of Adam and Eve, but I want to tell you what happened on that day in the Garden of Eden. If you don't mind, I want to use my spiritual imagination. Is that alright?

Adam and Eve were just hanging out in the garden and enjoying life. God had already given them the rules of the house, so to speak. They pretty much had free reign to do whatever they wanted, but there was one exception. There was one tree that they were not supposed to mess with.

It was kind of like the rules that you had in your house when you were growing up. There were some things that your parents told you not to mess with. Am I right? For instance, they told you not to mess with drugs. They told you not to mess with alcohol. They told you to stay away from certain kinds of people. Oh yeah, they told you what the rules were.

Adam and Eve were doing just fine until that old serpent came on the scene. The Bible says that the serpent was craftier than any of the wild animals that the Lord had created. In other words, he was slick. As a matter of fact, that was what some people called him, Slick.

Slick slid up to Eve one day and said, "Hey there, pretty Mama. Check out the fruit on that tree. Don't it look good?" Eve said, "Yeah, but God told us not to mess with that tree or we would die." However, Slick said, "You're not gonna die. God is just fooling you. He doesn't want you to have any fun. He knows that if you eat some of this fruit you will be as smart as He is. So come on. Take a bite."

You might have run into Slick before. He was the one that was always trying to get you to do things that were wrong when you were growing up and hanging out on the block. Eve went right ahead and listened to Slick and ate some of the forbidden fruit.

I think Eve knew that she had messed up. She knew that she was going to be in trouble. So, what do people do when they know that they have messed up? That's right. They try to persuade someone to mess up with them so they won't be in trouble by themselves, and it is usually one of their best friends. So she went and found Adam.

She said, "Hey Boo, I just had some of the fruit that is on that tree over there, and it is so good. Here, I save you some. Come on and take a bite", but Adam said, "Woman, are you crazy? God told us not to mess with that tree." Eve said, Come on Boo. **O.G.** is just trying to keep us from having any fun."

The Bible says that Adam went right ahead and disobeyed God too, and just like Eve, he knew that he had messed up. He knew that he had done wrong. He knew that he was in trouble. How do I know that? The Bible says that when they heard God coming they hid.

Let me ask you something. What did you used to do when you had done something that was wrong and you heard your parents or someone coming. That's right. Either you hid or you hid whatever it was that was going to get you into trouble. Am I right? So they hid.

God said, "Adam, where are you?" Adam replied, "We are hiding." God asked him, "Why are you hiding from me, Adam?" His answer was, "Because we are naked."

God said, "Who told you that you were naked? Adam, do you know what you have done? Because of your disobedience, sin has come into the world. Satan and all of his dogs have been let out to wreak havoc upon the world. So I ask you Adam. Who let the dogs out?

Our young men are always calling each other "dogs." They will say, "That's my dog." Well. I've got some news for you. Satan has some dogs too. Death is one of Satan's dogs. Sickness is one of Satan's dogs. Misery is one of Satan's dogs. Pain is one of Satan's dogs. Depression is one of Satan's dogs. Hopelessness is one of Satan's dogs. When Adam chose to disobey God, he opened up the gates of hell and let the dogs out on the world.

There was a song that came out a while back that was named, "The Atomic Dog." In it, the singer asked, "Why must I be like that? Why must I chase the cat? It's nothing but the dog in me."

Sometimes we do some of the dumbest things, and when someone asks us why we did it, we say, "I don't know." The truth is, sometimes we really don't know.

We look at society and wonder what is wrong with the world today. Crime is up. Drugs have taken over many of our neighborhoods. Mothers are pawning their children to drug dealers for another bag and grandmothers are selling their bodies for another rock. Our children have gone from singing, "Mary had a little lamb" to singing "Mary had a pimp." Somebody has let the dogs out.

Immorality has become fashionable. Homosexuality and lesbianism are now acceptable lifestyles. Our schools have become battlegrounds, and if we don't do something very soon, there will be more jails and prisons in this country than there are colleges and universities. Someone has let the dogs out.

Teachers are raping students. Priests are molesting young boys. Terrorist and suicide bombers are a constant threat all over the world. I'm telling you, somebody has let the dogs out.

The dogs have not only been let out in our schools and communities. They have been let out in our churches as well. That is why so many of our churches have become so ineffective. With the risk of offending some good church members, I want to tell you about some of the various kinds of dogs that have been let out among us.

The first type of dog that I want to talk about is **The Guard Dog**. Guard dogs are probably the most popular kind of dog there is. They are good at protecting your home as well as your family. If someone were to break into your house while you were away or asleep, a good guard dog will attack the intruder.

Guard dogs are, for the most part, territorial. The only time that they will attack someone is if that person were to go into his house, onto his property, or into his territory.

He will not go after a woman who is standing on the corner. He will not try to get to the gang bangers that are sitting on the porch across the street. He will not confront the neighborhood kids or the wino that is in the alley. As a matter of fact, a guard dog will not go anywhere looking for anyone. He will wait for them to come into his house, into his yard, into his territory, or into his comfort zone, and then he will be all over them.

You might not know it, but we have some guard dogs in our churches as well. Many of them are good Christians, but the problem is, they are territorial. They will not tell anyone about the goodness of the Lord outside of the safety and security of their church house. They will not talk to the woman that is standing on the corner. They will not reach out to the gang banger that is sitting on the porch across the street. They won't invite the neighborhood kids to Sunday school or offer the wino a better way of life. Instead, they will wait for them to come into the church, and then they will be all over them. We have to stop being guard dogs and venture outside of our comfort zones.

There is another kind of dog that I want to tell you about. It is **The Junkyard Dog.** Like the guard dog, the junkyard dog is very protective as well. He will fight or even die, trying to protect the stuff that is in the junkyard. However, the stuff that he is protecting is, for the most part, worthless. It is junk. That is what a junkyard is. It is where they store resalable junk. (Do you remember Sanford and Son?) That doesn't mean that the junk has no value at all. In some circumstances some of the things that are in the junkyard are usable, but to the junkyard dog, nothing is more valuable than what is in their junkyard.

I hate to tell you this, but we have some junkyard dogs in our churches as well. They are more concerned with tradition than they are with the Gospel. They care more about whose name you were baptized in rather than whose blood you were baptized in. They are more concerned with what a person wears to church than what is in his heart when he gets to church. They will fight you tooth and nail over tradition.

Their minds are made up and no one or nothing can change it. They don't care what the pastor says. They don't even care what the Bible says. They will say, "We never did it like that before." They don't realize that God doesn't care about tradition. It might have some value, but if it does not line up with His word, it is like that stuff that is in the junkyard. It is worthless. It is junk, and the people who fight the pastor to protect it, and are willing to split the church because of it, are nothing but junkyard dogs.

The next dog that I want to tell you about is **The Mad Dog.** Mad dogs have the virus disease that is called rabies. They call them mad because their disease makes them crazy. They get to the point where they can't stand anyone or anything. They want to attack everybody. If someone was to get too close to them, they will bite them, poisoning their system and passing their madness on to others.

I don't know if you realize it, but we have some mad dogs in our churches as well. They are always mad. They are mad at the pastor, mad at the deacons, mad at the choir, mad at the ushers and everybody else. They are full of anger and will express their anger to anyone who will listen to them. They will spread their poison throughout the congregation.

You have got to watch out for the mad dogs. They will come to you, talking about the pastor, the first lady, the Sunday school teacher, the choir director, the minister of music, the sound technician, the custodians, the parking lot attendants, the person who is sitting in their seat and everybody else that is in the church.

The next dog that you need to know about is **The Show Dog.** Show dogs are the ones that you see on television and in the movies. They are always looking good and competing with other dogs. They are usually pedigrees that are chosen from the best of the best, and they put on a real good show, but what else are they good for? They cannot protect your house. If someone were to break in, the burglar won't just take your stuff, he will take the dog too. The dog can't hunt or fight. All he can do is look good, do a few tricks and put on a good show. That is why they call them "Show dogs."

This might come as a surprise to you, but we have some show dogs in some of our churches too. They show up every Sunday and they look good. They put on a real good show. Some of them can even do a few tricks. What I mean is they can trick a few people. They can dance and shout with the best of them. They can talk "church talk" so well; you would think it was their major in college. Church talk.

What else can they do? They don't go to Bible study, prayer meetings or revivals. They never get involved in anything that the church is doing. So as a result, they never grow in the Lord. They can't even share their testimony about what the Lord has done for them. They are just Show Dogs.

The next dog that I want to talk about is every preacher's nightmare, **The Sleeping Dog.** Sleeping dogs do just that. They sleep. I know you have seen sleeping dogs portrayed on television or in the movies before. They are the ones that are normally stretched out on the front porch or in front of the fireplace.

No matter what is going on, he just lies there sleeping. Someone could be breaking into the house, and he just lies there sleeping. Someone in the house could be getting beat up or killed, and he just lies there sleeping. The house could be on fire, and he will just get up, move to a safe place, and then go back to sleep. Every once in a while he will raise his head, look around, stretch and yawn, and then he will put his head back down and go back to sleep.

I hate to have to be the one to tell you this, but there are some sleeping dogs in our churches as well. Preachers can take days preparing a sermon, and five minutes after he gets up to preach you can see heads bowed all over the church, and they are not praying.

Some people don't know this, but Satan has some demons that have only one job. That is to make you sleepy. Satan does not want you to hear God's word. That is why, when the choir is singing people will be on their feet, wide awake, but as soon as the preacher gets up, it's lights out. Sleeping dogs.

You can watch television all night long or read Ebony or Essence from cover to cover but when you pick up your Bible, your eyelids get so heavy that even Arnold Schwarzenegger couldn't lift them. Sleeping dogs.

The last type of dog that I want to talk to you about are **The Pack Dogs.** They are called pack dogs because these dogs usually run in packs. You very seldom see one of them alone. They are always hanging with other dogs. They are almost like a gang. If another dog, that is not part of the pack, tries to mingle with them, the pack will attack him. Everyone is intimidated by the pack dogs.

I hate to say it, but the church has some pack dogs too. We call them "clicks." No matter what auxiliary or ministry you are a part of, they have their clicks. The choir has their clicks. The ushers have their clicks. The deacons have their clicks. The preachers have their clicks. Even the bench members have their clicks.

Some of them get together like a pack of dogs and attack other church members that are not a part of their click. They sometimes intimidate other members, especially the newer ones, and make them feel uncomfortable and unwelcome. So they end up leaving the church because of the pack dogs.

We have to watch out for the *"BEWARE OF DOG"* signs. Too often, we ignore the signs that warn us of impending danger. Many of our emergency rooms are often times occupied by children and adults alike that have ignored the *"BEWARE OF DOG"* signs. Sometimes they have even seen the dog, but since he wasn't barking or growling at them, they thought he was safe to pet or play with.

I have another story for you. On a very cold evening, a young lady was walking through the woods on her way home. While she was walking she came across a snake that was lying by the side of the road. As she came closer she could see that the snake had been injured and was nearly frozen to death.

The woman felt compassion for the snake, so she picked him up, wrapped her coat around him and took him home with her. When she got home she fed the snake, placed him in front of the fireplace and nursed him all night long. The next morning, before she left for work, she changed his bandages, set plenty of food out for him and made sure the heat was left on high.

That evening, when she got home, she was surprised to see that the snake's wounds were healing and his condition was no longer critical. He was even crawling around on the floor, laughing and playing.

The woman was so happy that the snake was feeling better, she ran over to him, picked him up, and started hugging and kissing him. While she was hugging him, the snake hauled off and gave her a vicious bite on her neck.

The woman dropped the snake and fell back in a state of shock. She grabbed her neck, and with tears in her eyes she said, "How could you do this to me after all I have done for you. You know that your bite is poisonous and now I am going to die. How could you do this to me?"

Slick just looked at her and said, "Shut up, silly woman. You got just what you deserved. You knew I was a snake before you took me in."

Oh yeah, you have to watch out for the *"BEWARE OF DOG"* signs and understand that this is spiritual warfare that we are involved in, and Slick, also known as Satan, will do whatever he can to destroy you. There are no tricks that are beneath him and his dogs (demons), but I have some good news for you, my friend. You don't have to worry about the dogs, because one Friday evening on a hill called Calvary, Jesus hung on an old Roman cross dying for your sins and mine. While He hung there, all of the dogs were gathered around the cross. They had a party going on. They were dancing and howling and doing the atomic dog while they sang *"Who Let The Dogs Out."*

They partied all night Friday night, all day Saturday and all night Saturday night. Early that Sunday morning, Jesus stepped out of the grave with a leash in one hand and a muzzle in the other hand. He said, "I know who let the dogs out, but that doesn't matter now because all power is in my hands."

We have all sinned but Christ died for our sins. Now we have a choice. You can live with him forever or you can lie down and die with the dogs. *"For God so loved the world that He gave his only begotten Son, that whosoever believeth in Him shall not parish, but have ever lasting life. For God sent not His Son into the world to condemn the world; but that the world through Him might be saved." (John 3-16-17)*

CHAPTER TWELVE

Junkyard Jewel

Maya Azucena wrote and recorded a song that is so beautiful and powerful that the first time I heard it I almost cried. Maybe it touched me so deeply because it described me and so many other people that I know.

The name of the song is "Junkyard Jewel" and the lyrics are:

He was a Junkyard Jewel
Hidden in trash
Forgotten too long
Until found at last

Junkyard Jewel
With so much inside
Hidden from the rest
As a matter of pride

Until one day she came
And she saw in his eyes
She believed in him
Heard it through his cries

Bricks, beer, babies, glass
Anger, fear,
Now he rises above day by day
Until he is here

A Junkyard Jewel
Hidden in trash
Forgotten too long
Until found at last

She found him
He's broken
Alone in the fray
Believes in him
Even when he's lost his way

Saw the struggles, the strife
Saw the cut in his life
Saw potential, power
And the passion for life

He will rise above one day
Taking flight from the night
Into the light

Had his dreams dashed once
But they live on inside
Buried beneath
disappointment and lies

Now he builds dreams
For somebody else
Teaching those younger
That dreams are your wealth

A Junkyard Jewel
Hidden in trash
Forgotten too long
Until found at last

Junkyard Jewel
With so much inside
Hidden from the rest
As a matter of pride

Junkyard Jewel

You---Are---So---Beautiful

Can't you see?

Maya and her band went with me to the Medium Security Institution (The Workhouse) in St. Louis one day and she sang that song for the inmates there. I could tell that many of them were as moved as I was when I first heard it.

The world is full of junkyard jewels. They have lost their way and are living in a world of hopelessness. Some of them are in prison.

Some of them are on drugs. Some of them are prostitutes and some of them are in gangs. They are not bad people. Many of them are intelligent and talented, but they are victims of their environment.

Because of our culture, it seems that many of our young men and young boys believe that they have to live up to a certain image. It could be an image of toughness, shrewdness or sexual maturity, even at a young and tender age. They are exposed to unhealthy and sometimes even dangerous lifestyles everywhere they go; at school, at the malls, in the streets and sometimes even in their own homes. They grow up hearing that a man is not supposed to cry. They have to be tough. They must accept any appearance of a challenge, no matter what the odds are against them. The unwritten code of the streets is, **"NEVER BACK DOWN."**

You might not realize it, but Satan has put our young boys on his "hit list." He is trying to wipe them out and get rid of them just like he tried to get rid of another generation of young people, centuries ago.

You remember Moses, don't you? Satan realized that the Israelites were growing in numbers and they were becoming stronger as a people. So he figured that the only way to stop them was to kill off all of the young boys.

Have you noticed something? Whenever Satan decides to get rid of a generation of people, he always goes after the boys. He used Pharaoh to try to get rid of all of the baby boys by having the midwives kill them at birth. He said, *"When you help the Hebrew women in child birth and observe them on the delivery stool, if it is a boy, kill him; but if it is a girl, let her live. (Exodus 1:16 NIV)*

When that plan backfired, the Bible says that he ordered all of his people to throw every newborn boy into the Nile River, but Moses had a praying mother. She hid her baby as long as she could, and then she put him in a makeshift boat and carefully placed him in the river. When she placed her baby in the river that day, I believe what she was really doing was putting him in the hands of God.

Then Moses' sister went down to the river to watch out for her little brother. That is what we have to do more of these days. We need to watch out for our young people.

When I was a child, my friends and I couldn't get away with anything on Christiana (the street that we lived on) because of "The Heads." That was what we called my mother and her friends because their heads were always sticking out of their windows. All up and down the street there were heads popping in and out of windows.

There was Miss. Brown, Miss. Kate, Miss. Ella, Miss. Irene, Momma Doll, Miss. Brooks and my mother, Miss Mary (That was how we addressed them), but they were not just watching us, they were also watching over us.

That is what we need more of in our neighborhoods today. We need some heads, because Satan is after our young people. Just like the Israelites, he sees that we are growing stronger as a people. We are growing stronger educationally. More and more of our young men and women are graduating from colleges and universities than ever before.

We are growing stronger politically. African Americans are mayors of cities that at one time we were not even allowed to vote in. We are represented in every level of government, from the White House all the way down to the smallest municipality.

We are growing stronger economically. We have made major strides in the business world. We can afford to live anywhere we choose. It looks like Dr. Martin L. King's dream is finally becoming a reality. Not only that, more and more of us are beginning to realize our dreams as well.

However, Satan wants to shatter those dreams and destroy us as a people, but the only way he can do that is to kill off our young boys. This time he is not using a Pharaoh to kill them off. This time he is using the gangs to kill them off. This time he is using drugs to kill them off. This time he is using prison to kill them off. This time he is using peer pressure to kill them off. This time he is even using them to kill themselves off.

When Pharaoh gave the order to throw the little boys into the river, he wasn't just talking to his soldiers and henchmen. Exodus 1:22 says that he gave the order to all of his people.

Satan has declared war on our young boys, but this time he is not just sending a few people at them. This time he is sending everybody at them. He is sending the dope man at them. He is sending the hoochie mamas at them. He is sending the player haters at them. He is sending the unscrupulous advertisers at them. He is sending the apathetic schoolteachers at them. He is sending the blood thirsty policemen at them. He is sending an unfair justice system at them. He is even sending some of our own people at them.

There are a growing number of households where there is no male presence. Young mothers are struggling to raise their children all by themselves because the fathers are either dead, on drugs, in prison or they have abandoned their families because they don't know how to be fathers.

They know how to be daddies. As a matter of fact, that is what their wives and girlfriends call them, "My baby's daddy", but they have no idea how to be fathers. Many of them don't know how to be fathers because they were raised in homes where there was no father. The mother or grandmother was the head of the household.

There are some households where the man is present, but the woman is still considered to be the head of the house. Sometimes it is because the man is not willing to act like a man by stepping up to the plate and assuming his responsibilities. They would rather run the streets all night long, hanging out with the boys and spending their money on primos, blunts and 40s instead of staying home with their families and buying milk, bread and pampers. Unfortunately, I was one of them.

There are some cases where the man is doing the best that he can, but the woman is still considered to be the head of the house because she has a better job or makes more money than her husband, and sometimes she is quick to remind him of it. She will tell him, "I don't need you. I run this." After a while the man starts feeling intimidated or inferior.

Now, I'm not trying to make excuses for the brothers, but there is a segment in America that will hire black women, but they will not hire a black man, at least not on any good paying jobs. I believe that this is a deliberate and underhanded ploy, designed by Satan, to demoralize our young men and tear our families apart. Many of our black men have become disenfranchised and they have simply given up, but you don't have to take my word for it. Just look around. On any given day in many urban cities you will find hundreds of African American men that are between the ages of 18 and 55 that are standing idly and aimlessly on city street corners. Such hopelessness will eventually lead to criminal activity, prison or an early grave. Many of these disengaged men provide no financial support or nurture for their children.

Our young boys are witnessing this on a regular basis. They see the hurt. They see the pain. They see the brokenness. They look around and all they see is a world of hopelessness. That is why so many of them have given up before they have even tried. They are Junkyard Jewels.

Now, let's just take a look at the criminal justice system in America. There are almost one million African Americans in prison today. Blacks are 12% of this nation's population but we are almost 50% of the prison population. Black males are born with a 25% chance of going to prison sometime during their lifetime.

In her song, Maya Azucena talked about the struggles and strife of men, but men are not the only Junkyard Jewels. Since 1990, the number of female prisoners has increased by 106% and the numbers of children whose mothers are in prison have almost doubled since 1991. Now the fastest growing population in the prison system is young black women.

Many of them become pregnant before they finish high school. Some of them have low self-esteem because they are constantly being physically and mentally abused by one man after another. Some of them are jumping in and out of cars, selling their bodies because they are strung out on crack.

I believe it was Rev. Jesse Jackson who said that African Americans are no more criminal than anyone else in this society. Yet, for as long as this country has existed, blacks have gone through this nation's criminal justice system and have always been found wanting.

This system is unfair to African Americans primarily, and to other ethnic minorities generally. It does not matter what system we live under. If it is contaminated with bias, prejudices, and preconceived notions, then that system cannot function fairly.

Dr. King said, "There is nothing more dangerous than to build a society with a large segment of people in that society who feel that they have no stake in it; who feel that they have nothing to lose. People, who have a stake in their society, protect that society, but when they don't have a stake in it, they unconsciously want to destroy it."

Many of our young men and young women feel that they have no stake in this society. They have become disenfranchised. They have no jobs and they see no future. They are Junkyard Jewels.

Many of our ancestors gave their lives, fighting for the right to vote, but today, 14% of African Americans in this country have lost their right to vote and another 14% feel that they have nothing to vote for. They are Junkyard Jewels.

In the 6th Chapter of the Gospel of Mark, beginning at verse 32, Jesus was surrounded by crowds of hurting people. Some of them were sick. Some of them were blind. Some of them were crippled. Some of them were poor. Some of them were homeless. They were tired and hungry. Their feet were sore and their brows were filled with sweat from the heat of the noon day sun. Still, they came to Jesus because they were tired of their situation and they were looking for help.

This country is full of people who are lost and hurting. Drugs have taken over our communities. Unemployment is at an all time high. Food pantries cannot keep up with the demand. Thousands of families are without gas or electricity because they cannot afford to pay their utility bills.

Many of our senior citizens have to choose between buying food and buying the medicines that they need. Scores of children are suffering from all kinds of sicknesses and diseases, and their families can do nothing about it because they have no health care. Far too many of our young people are being exposed to first-class jails and second-class schools.

Just like the people that came to Jesus that day, they are sick, they are tired and they are looking for help, but the Bible says that after a while, the disciples said to Jesus, "Send them away." They wanted Jesus to send the people away so they could go to the surrounding villages and buy themselves something to eat. In other words, let them find help somewhere else, but Jesus said, "They don't need to go away. You give them something to eat."

Today, more and more people are coming to the church. The sick are coming. The hungry are coming. The alcoholics are coming. The drug addicts are coming. The gang bangers are coming. Men and women who have just gotten out of prison are coming. They are all coming to the church and they are looking for help.

What is the church's response? Just like the disciples, we are saying, "Send them away. We don't want those people with AIDS coming in here infecting the rest of us. Send them away. We don't want those crack heads and drunks in here with our children. Send them away. We don't want those homeless people coming in here smelling up our church. Send them away. We don't want those jailbirds and gang bangers coming in here starting trouble, pastor. Send them away."

The church is looking at a world full of lost and hurting people who are coming to us for help, but we are saying, "Send them away. They can get help somewhere else." I can hear Jesus saying, loud and clear, "They don't need to go away. You help them. These people are my Junkyard Jewels."

CHAPTER THIRTEEN

Children of the Night

In 1972, The Stylistics recorded a song entitled, "Children of the Night." Some of the lyrics were:

Late at night
When all the world is safe within their dreams
I walk the shadows
Late at night
An empty feeling creeps within my soul
I feel so lonely
So I go
Into the darkness of the night
All alone
I walk the until I find
Someone who is just like me
Looking for some company

Children of the night

Late ate night
A restless feeling takes control of me
And I can't fight it
Late at night
I feel the need for someone, who like me
Needs understanding
So once again
I'll search the darkness of the night
All alone
I'll walk each street until I find
Someone who is just like me
Looking for some company

Children of the Night

I was visiting the home of my friends, Vernon and Zetta Williams on Thanksgiving in 2002 when Vernon played that song. He loved dusties (Old School) and he had a large collection of them.

While the record was playing, I sat back on the couch with my eyes closed. Although I had heard that song many times before, it was as if I was hearing the words for the first time. I could visualize myself, years before, when I was stung out on drugs and living in a world of hopelessness. There were so many nights that I walked the streets in search of my kind of people, other addicts and hustlers. Other children of the night.

I walked the streets, sometimes all night long, looking for another hit, another drink, another woman or another party. I loved the night life. As a matter of fact, one of my favorite songs was, "Give me the night" by George Benson. That was my anthem. I was truly one of the children of the night.

Looking back, I now realize that, like so many others, I was living in a world of darkness. I was lost but I didn't know it. I thought I was having fun. So what if I went to jail from time to time. That was just an occupational hazard. So what if I was living a dangerous lifestyle. I wasn't going to live forever anyway. So what if I was hurting the people that cared about me. They'd get over it. If they didn't, then so what?

Delester Jefferson, President of the Laymen for the Berean Missionary Baptist District of Missouri, told a story about the time his organization took a group of children to Six Flags. One of the little boys got separated from the group and was lost. Delester found a security officer and told him that one of the children was lost. The officer asked, "Does the boy know that he is lost?" Delester was confused by the question. The officer explained that until the boy realizes that he is lost, he will just blend in with the rest of the children that were in the park.

Sure enough, when the little boy ran out of tickets he looked around for his group. When he didn't see any of them he became frightened and started crying. Then someone took the frightened little boy to one of the security officers and he was reunited with his group, but none of that happened until the little boy realized that he was lost.

A lot of people are lost but they don't know it. They think that all of the stuff that they are experiencing is just a part of life. They think going to jail is just a part of life. They think doing drugs is just a part of life. They think prostitution is just a part of life. They think being abused is just a part of life. They think gang banging is just a part of life. The truth is, none of that is a part of the life that God desires for you. That is how Satan wants you to live and think. Jesus said, *"The thief does not come except to steal, and to kill, and to destroy. I have come that they may have life, and that they may have it more abundantly."* *(John10:10)*

The prison system has become the fastest growing business in America. Currently, there are more than 2 million men and women that are filling our jails and prisons.

Many of our politicians and government officials are lining up to show their constituents they are "tough on crime". As a result, more and more people are being locked away for longer and longer periods of time. Society has given up on them. However, there is another segment of the population that society has given up on. They are the alcoholics, the poor, the homeless, the destitute, and the mentally ill.

We look down on them and say they no longer have a right to the American dream. They had their chance and they blew it. Now they are the outcast, the despised, and the eyesores of the community. What makes it worse is many of them have given up on themselves. If that were not bad enough, many of our churches have given up on them too. Now they are the ones that are filling many of our jails and prisons.

This is spiritual warfare that we are involved in. Satan hates God and he hates you because God loves you. He is going to hell to suffer eternally and he wants to take you with him. He does not want you to know that you are lost. He wants to keep you in the dark. He wants you to continue being one of his children of the night.

CHAPTER FOURTEEN

Can Anything Good Come Out Of Prison?

The prison industry is the fastest growing business in America. For centuries, we have been known as the land of the free, but for more than 2 million men and women, those words are just another line from a very old song. In many of our penal institutions, there is no such thing as rehabilitation. They have simply become cheap labor camps.

In many cases, it is not the fault of those who are in charge of the prisons. They are just doing their jobs, so we can't really blame them. Neither can we blame the parole boards for keeping these men and women locked away longer than necessary.

We can't blame the prosecutors who will do whatever it takes to win a conviction even if he or she knows that the defendant is not guilty. We cannot blame the judges for handing out all of those ridicules sentences. We can't even blame the police officers who will lie and plant evidence on someone so he can make an arrest.

Then who can we blame? Whose fault is it that this nation has become so cold hearted, blood thirsty and unforgiving?

Well, this might come as a shock to you, but I blame the church. Yes I do. I blame the church because there are too many of us that just don't care what happens in this country as long as it doesn't affect us. We don't care how unfair this justice system is, as long as our families are not caught up in it.

It doesn't bother us that so many of our sons and daughters have become victims of the crack epidemic, just as long as our children are not strung out. Some of us can even sit in our nice, warm cars while on our way to church, and see a homeless person that is obviously cold and hungry, and just turn our heads as it they didn't exist. We can look at an entire generation of young people being drug off to prison and not even care.

If it sounds like I'm a little angry right now, I am. I'm angry because our juvenile justice system is outgrowing the juvenal educational system. I'm angry because more than 10% of our young black men who are between the ages of 25 and 29 are in prison right now and nobody cares.

Most of all, I'm angry because the church has lost its compassion for those who are lost, and has bought into societies philosophy of, "Lock em up and throw away the key."

Don't get me wrong. I'm not saying that there shouldn't be any jails or prisons. That is where some people need to be. What I am saying is prison should not be the solution to every problem that we don't have an answer.

We can't keep throwing all of these men, women, and now even little children into these deep, dark, dungeons of despair with no hope of ever seeing the light of day again. I don't care what anybody says. It's just wrong.

Oh yeah, I'm angry right now. I'm angry because thousands of men and women are being released from prison every year with no money, no home to go to, and no one to turn to for help. Many of them are trying their best to do what's right, but no one will give them a chance. Not even some of our churches. They are afraid of them. They don't trust them. They don't want them in their churches. They're asking themselves, "Can anything good come out of prison."

Someone told the story about a church that was located in a bad neighborhood. Every Sunday while worship services were going on, all of the doors were kept locked. One day someone asked the pastor why they kept the doors locked during services. He said, "This neighborhood is full of sinners. We are surrounded by alcoholics, drug addicts, prostitutes, and people like that. If the doors are not locked, some of them might try to come in here."

In John 1:35, Jesus started assembling His first disciples. Peter and Andrew and some of the boys had started following Him and they were excited because they had found the savior that everyone has been waiting for. Philip was so excited, he went and found Nathaniel and told him that they had found the one that Moses and the prophets written about, Jesus of Nazareth.

Look at Nathaniel's response. *"Can anything good come out of Nazareth?"* *(Verse 46 NAS)* What made him say something like that? What was wrong with being from Nazareth?

Well, for one thing, being a frontier town contributed to the reputation that Nazareth was not an important part of the national or religious life of Israel. It was also known for its bad reputation when it came to moral values and religion.

In other words, it was not where the right people came from. It was on the other side of the tracks. It was in the projects, so to speak. It was the ghetto, the slums. It was a place where people were not expected to succeed.

In today's society, Nazareth would be filled with inadequate and over-crowed schools. It would have a liquor store on every corner and a crack house in every block. The neighborhoods would be lined with abandoned buildings and the streets would be full of young men with their pants hung low and their caps on backwards.

So, what about Nathaniel? How could he make a statement like that? How could he just write off an entire population of people as being no good? Nathaniel grew up in the church. He knew the scriptures. He worshiped in the temple every Saturday with all of the other church folks.

When he heard that Jesus was from Nazareth, he made up his mind that God couldn't have sent Him, because as far as he was concerned, nothing good could come out of Nazareth.

People have a way of categorizing other people and putting them in groups and saying they are all just alike. Some of them are categorized by race and others by their occupation. Some are categorized by their religion, or lack there of. In St. Louis, people are categorized by what high school they went to. Jesus was categorized by where he had come from.

You need to hear this. When Philip told Nathaniel about Jesus, he addressed him as "Jesus of Nazareth." So he immediately placed Jesus in the category with everybody else that came from Nazareth. It is important that you hear this because the church has been known to categorize people too. Yes we do.

We categorize them as gang bangers. We categorize them as drug addicts. We categorize them as prostitutes. We categorize them as a lost generation. We have distanced ourselves from them and we have completely and totally written them off.

The story was told of a very bad man that died one day and went before the judgment throne. Before him stood Abraham, David, Peter, and Luke. A chilly silence hung heavy in the room as an unseen voice began to read the details of the man's life. There was nothing good that was recorded. When the voice concluded, Abraham spoke. "Men like you cannot enter the Heavenly kingdom." He said. "You must leave."

"Father Abraham," the man cried, "I do not defend myself. I have no choice but to ask for mercy. Certainly, you understand. Though you lied to save your own life, saying your wife was your sister, by the grace and mercy of God you became a blessing to all nations."

David interrupted, "Abraham has spoken correctly." He said. "You have committed evil and heinous crimes. You do not belong in the kingdom of light." The man faced the great king and cried, "Son of Jesse, it is true. I am a wicked man. Yet I dare ask you for forgiveness. You slept with Uriah's wife and later, to cover your sin, arranged his death. I ask only forgiveness as you have known it."

Peter was next to speak. "Unlike David, you have shown no love to God. By your acid tongue and your vile temper you have wounded the Son of God." "I should be silent," the man muttered. "The only way I have used the blessed name of Jesus is in anger. Still, Simon, son of Jonah, I plead for grace. Though you walked by his side and listened to words from his own lips, you slept when he needed you in the garden, and you denied him three times in his night of greatest need."

Then Luke the Evangelist spoke. "You must leave. You have not been found "worthy of the kingdom of God." The man's head bowed sadly for a moment before a spark lit his face. "My life has been recorded correctly," the man began slowly. "I am guilty as charged. Yet I know there is a place for me in this blessed kingdom."

"Abraham, David, and Peter will plead my cause because they know of the weakness of man and the mercy of God. But you, blessed physician, will open the gates to me because you have written of God's great love for the likes of me. Don't you recognize me, Luke? I am the lost sheep that the Good Shepherd carried home; I am your younger, prodigal brother." The gates opened, and Luke embraced the sinner.

Can anything good come out of Nazareth? Can anything good come out of the projects? Can anything good come out of the slums and ghettos of our cities? Can anything good come out of prison?

CHAPTER FIFTHTEEN

Taking the City for God

This chapter was inspired by my pastor, Rev. Dr. Ronald L. Bobo, Sr. Actually, "Taking The City For God" is the mission statement of West Side Missionary Baptist Church, where I am a member. That is what God has commissioned us to do, but that charge was not only given to West Side. It was given to every church and every Christian. Our mission is to take back all of our cities from the enemy, who is Satan.

Many of our churches have gotten away from instruction. Therefore, far too many church members fail to understand what Christianity really means. As a result, more and more of our churches have merely become social clubs.

We are soldiers in the army of the Lord, am I right? At least, that's what we say we are, but what kind of soldiers are we? Moreover, what kind of recruits are we producing? Are they some of those "Good soldiers" that the Apostle Paul talked about? Or are they more like "weekend warriors," reservists who only serve on weekends.

During my teenage and my young adult years, I saw many of my friends leaving home, heading for the battlefields of Vietnam. Some of them went into the Marine Corp, where they served their country well by fighting in the hills, in the valleys and in the trenches.

Some time later I enlisted in the Marine Corp myself. Now, that may lead you to believe that I was one of those "Good Soldiers" during my years of military service. By good soldiers, I mean one of those soldiers that could not wait to get to the battlefield and engage in mortal combat with the enemy. I mean one of those soldiers who was not afraid to go into enemy territory. I mean one of those soldiers whose main objective was taking the city by any means necessary.

Well, I'm sorry to disappoint you, but the truth is, I was not one of those soldiers. Not me. You see, although the Vietnam war was going on when I joined the marines, that was not the reason I joined. Even with all of my military and my combat training, they still could not make me believe that that was my war too.

I just could not see myself leaving my comfort zone, to go off to some distant and unfamiliar battlefield. Myself, and so many others felt that it was not our job to go. After all, didn't they have professional soldiers for that? What about the Green Beret, the Recon

Rangers or the Navy Seals? You know, those real soldiers. That was their job. Let them go.

Don't get me wrong. We were not unpatriotic concerning the war effort. We were more than willing to defend our country. Just let those Viet Cong come marching down State Street or Madison Avenue. Then everybody would see just how patriotic we really were. We did not have a problem with defending our country. We just did not want to go into enemy territory to do it.

Many of our churches and church members have that same mentality. Just look at some of the soldiers that have enlisted into God's army. They sit in church Sunday after Sunday and hear God's Word being preached over and over again. Still, many of them are not willing to leave their comfort zones and go into enemy territory. Am I right about it?

They say, "Don't they have professional Christians for that? That's the pastor's job, or that's the deacon's job, or let the outreach people do that."

There is a war going on out there, and day after day we see the casualties of that war. Drug addicts are casualties of that war. Alcoholics are casualties of that war. Prostitutes are casualties of that war. Gang bangers are casualties of that war. Abused children are casualties of that war. Our jails and prisons are full of casualties of that war.

Just like the Vietnamese were helpless, and they needed the United States to go over there and take the city from the Viet Cong, the sinners in our streets are helpless, and they need the church to go out there and take this city from Satan.

Us church folk are going to have to leave our comfort zones, put on the whole armor of God, and get out there on the battlefields. Your job is the battlefields. Your school is the battlefield. Your neighborhood is the battlefields. Where ever there are lost souls, that is the battlefield.

Too many of us want to stay in the church house and wait for the people to come to us, then we will witness to them and tell them all about the goodness of the Lord from the safety of our pews. The truth is, we cannot take the city unless we go into the City.

When I joined the Marines, I joined for selfish reasons. Yes I did. I joined for one reason and one reason only. I didn't want to go to jail. That was it. I knew that I had messed up. So I figured that the best way to stay out of jail was to join the military.

I didn't join the Marines because I loved my country. It was not because I wanted to be a Marine, and it was not because I wanted to help those countries that could not help themselves. I was not concerned with what was going on overseas. I didn't even want to go overseas. I just didn't want to go to jail. However, I ended up going to jail anyhow, because I was doing the same stuff after I joined the Marines that I was doing before I joined the Marines.

There are some people in our churches today that have that same attitude. They are there for selfish reasons. The only reason that some of them joined the church is because they don't want to go to hell.

They did not join the church because they love the Lord, and they did not join because they want to be a Christian. It is certainly not because they want to reach those who are lost, because they are not concerned with what's going in the streets of our cities, as long as it doesn't affect them.

They joined the church for one reason and one reason only. **_Fire Insurance._** They just don't want to go to hell. Well I want to serve notice on you. Some of them are going to end up in hell anyhow, because they are doing that same stuff after they joined the church that they were doing before they joined the church.

I've got a news flash for you. Contrary to popular belief, everybody that's in the church is not saved. You do know that don't you? Some of the people that are saved leave a lot to be desired. You remember the prodigal son's brother don't you? He became angry when his brother repented and went back home. Some folks that are in the church are the same way.

Let me tell you something else that might surprise you. Most sinners or most un-churched people don't have a problem with God, and they don't have a problem with the Bible. If the truth be told, they don't even have a problem with the church.

Most people that don't go to church have a problem with church folks. The reason some people don't go to church today is because of the way they were treated when they did go. Let me tell you something else while I'm on the subject. Some people don't go to church because they see how some of the people act that do go to church.

Most of the times, before an army sends in all of its troops, it will send in an advance party to check things out. In the 13th chapter of Numbers, God had Moses to send out an advance party to scout out the land that the Lord was going to give them, but when they returned, only two of the twelve had a good report. Only two were in favor of taking the city. That is only about 18%, better known as the faithful few.

The others said, "We can't fight those people. They are much stronger than we are." Therefore, they started murmuring and spreading rumors throughout the camp and casting doubt among the congregation saying, "Hey Dawg, Moses is crazy. He has lost his ever-loving mind. We can't take that city. We saw people there that were so big; they made us look like grasshoppers."

There may have been some times that you were asked to go out as advance parties too. Your pastor told you to go throughout the city and find those who are lost and hurting and tell them about the God who loves them.

Just like the children of Israel, some of the people started murmuring, saying, "Hey y'all. The pastor is crazy. He has lost his mind. We can't take this city. The gang bangers are too strong for us. The drug dealers are too strong for us. The crack heads are too strong for us."

So you ended up with the faithful few, but that's all right. God specializes in doing great things with a few. He took two fish and five loaves of bread and fed five thousand men, plus women and children. God specializes in doing great things with a few. He took three Hebrew boys and started a revolution in Babylon. God specializes in doing great things with a few. Jesus took twelve men and changed the world so much they are still talking about it 2,000 years later.

I'm telling you that God specializes in doing great things with a few. So don't get discouraged when you need some volunteers for a special project and only a few people show up. God specializes in doing great things with a few.

Let me move along to the battle itself. When it came time to take the city of Jericho, God had Joshua to use a very peculiar strategy. He instructed them to do only two things: March and Shout. That was the battle plan. You don't have to take my word for it. It's right there in the text. Read the sixth chapter of the book of Joshua. First, they were to march, and then they were to shout.

He told them to march around the city with their army once a day for six days. Then on the seventh day, He said to march around the city seven times. He wanted them to march first.

Now, that seemed like a strange battle plan to me. However, after thinking about it, during my military training, when they were preparing us for warfare, the first thing they taught us was how to march.

They did not start by teaching us how to fire our weapons. Neither, did they start by teaching us hand-to-hand combat. All that came later. Their first objective was to take a platoon of individuals and train them to function as one body.

If the church is ever going to learn how to function as one body, we are going to have to learn how to march. Now bear with me for a just a few minutes while I try to explain this thing.

The military has six basic marches. After you learn one, then you move on to the next. The first march that you learn is called the mark-time march. The mark-time march is when you are going through the motions of marching but you are not going anywhere. You are moving your feet but you are never advancing. So no matter how long you march, or how tired you get, when you are mark-time marching, you will always be in the same place that you were when you first started marching, because you're just mark-time marching.

There are too many church folks who are mark-time marching. Sunday after Sunday, they are going through the motions but they are not getting anywhere. They are still in the same place, spiritually, that they were when they first got saved. Some of them have been in the church for 10, 20, 30 years or more.

They are just mark-time marching. They don't study their Bibles. They are just mark-time marching. They don't pray. They are just mark-time marching. They don't fast. They are just mark-time marching. So consequently, they are not growing in the Lord because, they are just mark-time marching.

The next march that they learn is called the quick-time march. The quick-time march is when everyone is marching along in the same step and the drill sergeant is calling cadence for you. Calling cadence is when the drill sergeant is saying, "Left-right-left. Left-right-left."

He is telling you when to step with your left foot, and he is telling you when to step with your right. He is telling you when to turn to your left, and he is telling you when to turn to your right. He is telling you when to go forward, and he is telling you when to stop.

You have got to listen carefully because there are some other platoons that are marching in the same area, and their platoon sergeants are calling cadence for them too. Therefore, if you are not listening carefully, you might hear their sergeant and think it is your sergeant and you end up going off in the wrong direction.

I just want to let you know that the Holy Ghost is calling cadence for you. He is saying "Left-right-left. Left-right-left." He is telling you when to step with your left foot and He is telling you when to step with your right. He is telling you when to turn to your left and He is telling you when to turn to your right. He is telling you when to go forward and He is telling you when to stop.

You've got to listen very carefully because Satan is out there, and he knows how to call cadence too. So if you are not listening carefully, and prayerfully, you might hear his voice, and think it is the Lord's voice, and you will go marching off in the wrong direction.

The third march is called double-time march. Most soldiers don't like the double-time march because oftentimes they have to run up some hills and through some valleys. Before the march is over, they are tired and sweaty, and their bodies are all racked with pain.

The purpose of the double-time march is to build your strength and your endurance. It also gives you more confidence in your unit, the sergeant knows when you have gone as far as you can go. So when you get to the point where you just can't take any more. When you feel like your legs are about to give out and you are about to pass out. When you are about ready to just throw up your hands and quit, the sergeant will hold up his hand and say, "Company, halt."

There will be times on your Christian journey when the Lord will say, "Double-Time March". He will let trouble come your way. He will let heartaches come your way. He will let pain come your way. He will let you go through some trials and some tribulations. You will be disappointed and you will have to cry sometimes, but that's just to make you stronger and to help build up your spiritual endurance, and increase your faith in God. I've got some good news for you. Jesus knows just how much you can bear. So before the load gets too heavy. When you are at the point where you just cannot take any more. When you are just about ready to give up. When you're about ready to just throw up your hands and quit. The Lord will hold up His Hand and say, "Trouble, halt."

The next march is called the half-step march. The half-step march could also be known as the show time march because you make all kinds of pretty noises with your feet. It draws attention to you because the noise sounds so good, but you have got to remember that when you are half-step marching, all you are really doing is just half-stepping.

Too many church folks are just half-stepping. They put on a real good show and they get people's attention because what they say sounds so good. They know when to say, "Halleluiah." They know when to say, "Amen." They know when to say, "Praise the Lord." Some of them are officers in the church or they are in charge of important ministries, but if the truth be told, they're just half-stepping.

They don't pay their tithes. They are just half-stepping. They don't attend revivals. They are just half-stepping. They don't tell anybody about the goodness of the Lord. They're just half-stepping. They don't put their trust in God. They are just half-stepping. That is why they are not growing in the Lord. They are just half-stepping.

The next march is called the, "To-the-rear march." The to-the-rear march is really very simple. You just turn around and go back where you came from. I think most of you already know where I am going with this one.

There are too many church folks who keep doing the "To-the-rear march." They keep going back to the same thing that God has delivered them from. They keep going back to the bars and taverns. They keep going back to the crack house. They keep going back to that woman's house, back to that man's house, back to the gambling house, back to the lying, back to the cheating, back to the stealing. Every time temptation comes their way, they do a **"To-the-rear march."**

The last march is called the forest march. The forest march is when you get into full combat gear. You put on your helmet. You put on your backpack. You put on your flack jacket. You put on your utility belt. You get your weapon and everything else you need and you march to the battlefield.

It is time to put on The Whole Armor of God and head to the battlefield, but remember, the march was only the first part of the battle plan. The next part was the shout. You must remember, God did not tell them to wait until the walls fell, to shout. He said, **"SHOUT**, and then the walls of the city will fall flat."

I feel another story coming on. There was a woman that was known in her local church as, "Shouting Mary." They called her that because Mary would shout at the drop of a hat. When the deacons started praying, Mary started shouting. When the choir started singing, Mary started shouting. When the pastor started preaching, Mary started shouting.

One day, Mary's house caught fire and burned to the ground. When Sunday morning rolled around, everyone at the church was talking about Mary's misfortune. They were saying, "I know old Mary is not going to shout this morning. She doesn't have anything to shout about. She has lost everything that she had." So everybody's eyes were on Mary. When the deacons started praying, old Mary started shouting. When the choir started singing, Mary started shouting. When the pastor started preaching, Mary started shouting.

After service was over, some of the people went over to Mary and asked her how could she still shout after loosing everything that she had? Mary said, "That's easy." She said, "When the deacons are praying their eloquent prayers, I look at them and I see Jesus. Then I shout. When the choir is singing the songs of Zion, I look at them and I see Jesus. Then I shout. When the pastor is preaching the Word of God, I look at him and I see Jesus. Then I shout, and when "old man trouble" comes my way, I look *around* him and I see Jesus. Then I shout."

Then she said, "I once was young, but now I'm old. I have never seen the righteous forsaken or His seed beg for bread. So I don't have to wait 'till the battle is over. I don't have to wait 'till the victory is won. I can shout now."

Let me tell you something. You don't have to wait until the battle is over, before you shout. You don't have to wait until the victory is won, before you shout. You don't have to wait until God heals your body before you shout. You don't have to wait until God saves your children, before you shout. You don't have to wait until God delivers you from whatever you're going through, before you shout.

If you have trouble at home, you can shout now. If you have trouble on your job, you can shout now. If you have trouble in your school, you can shout now. If you have problems with your health, you can shout now.

You don't have to wait until the walls fall down before you shout. God said, "**SHOUT,** and then the walls will come tumbling down"

CHAPTER SIXTEEN

Hold On. Help Is On the Way

I will lift up mine eyes unto the hills from whence cometh my help. My help cometh from the Lord, which made Heaven and earth. (Psalms 121: 1-2)

This particular Psalm has a very special place in my heart. It was one of two Psalms that my father taught me. The first Psalm that he taught me was the 23rd Psalm. He taught me that when I was very young and didn't know anything about the Lord. I didn't know who God was, or should I say who God is, and I had no idea how much He loved me.

My father wanted me to know just who my shepherd really was. So he opened his Bible to the 23rd Psalm and showed me where it says, "The Lord is my Shepherd"

You see, he did not want me to be confused about this thing. He wanted me to know exactly who my shepherd was because he wanted to make sure that I knew who it was that I was supposed to follow. He wanted me to know that the neighborhood gang leader was not my shepherd. He wanted me to know that the corner drug dealer was not my shepherd. And as much as my father loved me, although he would do anything that he could for me, he wanted me to know that not even he was my shepherd. So he sat me down one day and said, "Son, the Lord is your shepherd."

However, several years later I backslid, turning my back on God and walking away from His church. I became an alcoholic with a heroin and cocaine habit that was costing me an average of $200.00 a day. My drug habit led me into a life of crime. I was in and out of trouble, in and out of jails and prisons all across this country. I was living a life that was full of misery and pain. I knew I was in trouble and I desperately wanted somebody to help me, but I did not know where to go to find it.

So once again, I went to my father. And once again he opened his Bible, but this time it was to the 121st Psalm. He showed me where it said, "I will lift up my eyes to the hills from whence comes my help. My help comes from the Lord who made Heaven and earth."

Then he said, "Son, whenever you need help, just look to the hills and call on the Lord, and if you really mean it, then all you've got to do is just hold on because help is on the way."

As you already know, Ralph, and I loved to watch cartoons when we were children. Every Saturday morning and every evening after school our eyes would be glued to the television set while we watched cartoons like Heckel & Jeckel, Bugs Bunny, Mighty Mouse and Mr. Magoo. Do you remember them?

However, my favorite cartoon of them all was Popeye. The more I think about it, the more I am convinced that our churches would be much stronger if our members were more like Popeye. One thing I learned from watching Popeye was that he knew exactly where his help came from. Oh yeah, he knew without any doubt what gave him his strength. It was his spinach. Am I right?

So when he came up against something that he could not handle, he didn't get all worried and depressed. He just said, "That's all I can stands, cause I can't stands no more." Then he reached into his bosom and pulled out a can of spinach. Here is the good part. Before he had eaten it, before he had even opened the can, he knew that everything was going to be all right because he knew where his help came from.

Too many church folks do not know where their help comes from. They read their horoscope every morning looking for help. They call their psychic friends looking for help. They are standing in the lottery lines looking for help. They go to the boats and to the casinos looking for help. They turn to Oprah and Dr. Phil looking for help, but Jesus said, *"I will pray to the Father and He will give you another helper that He may abide with you forever."* (John 14:16)

The Holy Spirit is the one who Jesus called to be by your side, to help you, to stand by you, to strengthen you and to assist you.

Another thing I learned about Popeye was that he had a fresh supply of spinach every day. That leads me to believe that every morning before he left home he went to his supply source and got his spinach for the day because he knew that Brutus was going to be out there somewhere trying to catch him off guard. So, Popeye did not depend on yesterday's spinach to get him through today's battles, and he did not depend on the spinach that he had had when he first became a sailor. He knew that he had to have a fresh supply of spinach everyday.

We as Christians are going to have to learn to ask God for a fresh anointing of His Holy Spirit everyday. Ephesians 5:18 says, "Be filled with the Spirit." In the original Greek, "Be filled" means to keep on being filled, constantly and continually.

You cannot be satisfied with yesterday's filling, and you can't be satisfied with the filling that you received when you first got saved. Therefore, you ought to be like Popeye. Every morning, before you leave your house, you ought to get down on your knees and go to your supply source, and get a fresh filling of the Holy Spirit.

So when you are going through your daily routine and the cares of the world are starting to take its toll on you. When you don't have but one nerve left, and Satan is getting on that one. When you feel like you are at the end of your rope and you just can't take any more. You can do like Popeye, and say, "That's all I can stands, cause I can't stands no more."

Then you can reach down in your bosom, way down in the depths of your soul, and you can call on your supply source, which is Jesus Christ. Then after you call on Him, all you have to do is just hold on because help is on the way.

Another thing that I really admired about Popeye was the fact that he wanted everybody to know where his help came from. He was not ashamed to tell people that it was his spinach that gave him is strength. As a matter of fact, he had a song that praised his spinach. You heard that song before.

"I'm Popeye the sailor man
I'm Popeye the sailor man
I'm strong to the finish,
cause I eats me spinach
I'm Popeye the sailor man."

I know you heard that song before. He sang it all of the time. When the show came on, he would be singing his song and praising his spinach. While he was walking down the street, he would be singing his song and praising his spinach. Everywhere he went he was singing his song and praising his spinach, and while he was singing his song, he had a smile on his face and joy in his heart because he was so glad to be able let the world know how much he loved his spinach.

We ought to be like Popeye, but there are too many church folks who sit in God's house Sunday after Sunday looking like they are mad at the world. They won't praise the Lord and they get mad at you if you want to praise Him. They won't stand up. They won't clap their hands. They won't pat their feet. They won't even smile. The choir or praise team could be singing their hearts out, trying to lead the church in praise and worship while they are just sitting there looking at their watches and saying, "I'll be glad when they sit down and stop making all that noise. It don't take all that", but we have got to learn how to praise the Lord and thank Him for what He has done and for what we have, instead of always complaining about what we don't have. Haven't God been good to you? Did He wake you up this morning? Did He put food on your table? Did He put a roof over your head? Well praise Him.

However, I have a confession. I am not always as thankful as I should be either. I was released from prison after serving 10 months of a two-year sentence. While I was incarcerated, God got my attention through a prison evangelist, named Rev. Jerry Hodges. I gave my life to the Lord and started going to church regularly. I also continued my education, scoring number one in my GED class. I like to tell people that I was class valedictorian of the state penitentiary. I even completed a few college courses before I was released.

When I got out of prison, I decided to go to church on the first Sunday of my freedom. The church was approximately three miles away, and since all I had was one dollar to my name, I decided to walk there and ride the bus back. It was a very, very hot August day. It was so hot that even the flies were walking, and using their little wings to fan themselves.

While I was walking, I started thinking about the car that I had had before I went to prison. It had been repossessed while I was locked down. The further I walked, the hotter I got. The hotter I got, the more angry I became. I started complaining because I had to walk in all of that heat.

In the distance behind me, I heard someone that was singing and whistling as if he didn't have a care in the world. As he got closer, I started getting angry with him. I said to myself, "Why is this fool so dog gone happy as hot as it is out here? I'm walking in all of this heat, and he is back there singing and whistling and making all of that dog gone noise."

I became so angry; I turned around so I could see who this nut was that was so happy. What I saw completely blew my mind. It was a man with no legs, rolling along in a wheel chair with a big smile on his face. As he rolled past me, he greeted me politely, commented about the lovely weather, and kept right on singing.

I really felt ashamed of myself. There I was with two good legs, complaining because I had to walk. I learned to praise God regardless of my circumstances. I don't care how bad off you think you are, there is always somebody who is worse off than you are. So praise God for what you have.

Now, I really need you to help me out with something. There is something that I have been confused about for a long time. I have always wondered why no one would eat any spinach except Popeye. Did you ever wonder about that?

I mean, every time someone got into trouble, they would call Popeye and he would eat some spinach and then rescue them. Why didn't they just eat some spinach themselves? Could it be that they didn't know what spinach was?

Well, Ralph, and I decided to try something one day. In my old neighborhood, there was a bully whose name was Fat Nash. You might remember me talking about him in "The Hoodlum Preacher."

Fat Nash had the entire neighborhood terrorized. I mean, a bunch of us could be in the alley playing ball, but if someone said that Fat Nash was coming, the whole alley would clear out in no time flat. Even the dogs in the neighborhood were scared of Fat Nash. They wouldn't even bark at him. If that wasn't bad enough, he had a big brother that was called, Big Nash.

One day, Ralph and I decided to eat some spinach and then go and beat up Fat Nash, and if Big Nash was there, we were going to beat him up too. We almost tore up our pillows one night, practicing on them. That Saturday morning when we were at the grocery store with my mother, we told her that we wanted some spinach, a lot of it.

Now that surprised my mother because she knew that we didn't like greens. When we got back from the store and started looking for the spinach, it surprised us even more, because we didn't know that spinach was greens. It didn't look like greens when Popeye ate it.

When we asked my mother where the spinach was, she pointed to the greens. I yelled out, "That ain't no spinach. Them greens!" She said, "What do you think spinach is?" Needless to say, we didn't eat the spinach, and we didn't mess with Fat Nash either.

I told you that, to tell you this. There are so many people in the church, who are confused as to who the Holy Spirit really is. They do not know that He is God. They just see somebody who will shout all over the church on Sunday and then turn right around and curse everybody out on Monday. They'll say, "If that is what it means to be filled with the Spirit, then I don't want it."

What they don't realize is, if they are not filled with the Spirit, they are missing out on a lot of God's blessings, because without God's Spirit, you cannot love those who do not love you. Without God's Spirit, you cannot have the joy of the Lord. Without

God's Spirit, you cannot have peace in the time of trouble. Without God's Spirit, you will not have the patience to wait on the Lord. I'm telling you, you have to be filled with the Spirit.

Let us look into the lives of some of the people in Popeye's world that chose not to eat spinach.

First of all, there was Olive Oyl. You remember Olive Oyl don't you? She was Popeye's girlfriend. Now, Olive Oyl was not a bad person. She was kind of skinny and funny looking, but she was a very nice and pleasant young lady.

Her problem was that she would fall for every trick that Brutus came at her with. She used to make me so mad because Popeye would be trying to warn her. He would be begging her, saying "Olive, don't go there. Olive, don't do that", but Olive Oyl just would not listen. She would go right ahead, following after Brutus and believing his lies until she found herself in something that she could not get out of.

Christians who are not filled with the Spirit are the same way. They will fall for every trick that Satan comes at them with. Other Christians will be trying to warn them, saying, "You shouldn't be hanging out with that crowd. You know they don't mean you any good."

Aw yeah, they try to warn them, saying, "Look here brother. You shouldn't be going to those places. You are going to get caught up in that same old stuff again." Or, "Look here sister. You better watch that man. You know he doesn't care about you. He's just trying to get you into bed."

Inevitably, just like Olive Oyl, some of you won't listen. You go right ahead, following after Satan and believing his same old lies. Pretty soon, you start reminiscing and thinking about some of the things that you used to do, and some of the places that you used to go, and some of the people that you used to run with before you got saved.

Then Satan really starts talking to you. He's says, "That stuff that you used to do wasn't all bad. You really did have some good times back then. You just went too far. You can do some of that stuff again"

Then it starts sounding good, so you start agreeing with him, saying "Yeah, I know that God delivered me from a life of drugs, but I was smoking crack back then. I'm just going to smoke a little weed this time." Or you'll say, "I know I was a hopeless drunk when Jesus saved me, but I'm not going to drink Jack Daniels this time. I'm just going to drink wine coolers from now on." Or you'll say, "I know that I almost lost my family when I was laying up with Billy Bob, or Susie Bell, but I'm not going to sleep with them this time. I'm just going over there to have dinner."

Before you know it, you're going to find yourself: in trouble again, pregnant again, strung out again, in Jail again, or without hope again. Then all you have to do is just call on the Lord again, repent of your sins again, and ask God to fill you with His Holy Spirit and then just hold on because help is on the way.

The next person that I want to tell you about was Wimpy. You remember Wimpy don't you? "I'll *gladly pay you Tuesday, for a hamburger today.*" He was the negotiator. He always wanted to eat first, and then he would pay for it later, if he had to.

You know what I found out. There are a lot of Wimpy's in the church too. They are always trying to make a deal with God. They want God to bless them first, and then they might do what He wants them to do.

I can hear them now, "Lord, I will gladly tithe, if you will give me a better job", or "Lord, I will start going to church every Sunday if you will just get me out of this mess that I'm in."

Aw, come on now. You know we have some Wimpy's in the church. They are the ones that are always praying those "I ain't gone do it no more" prayers.

Finally, there was Sweet Pea. Little Sweet Pea. When I used to watch Popeye, Sweet Pea was a little baby, crawling around, drinking his milk from a bottle, saying "Goo Goo" and "Gaa Gaa", and getting into all kinds of trouble because he didn't know any better. That was almost 50 years ago.

You know what I found out? I found out that Sweet Pea is still a little baby. He is still crawling around. He is still drinking his milk from a bottle. He is still saying, "Goo Goo" and "Gaa Gaa", and he is still getting into all kinds of trouble, because he still doesn't know any better, 50 years later.

You might not know it, but there are a lot of Sweet Peas in our churches today. Some of them have been saved 20, 30, 40 years or more, and they are still babes in Christ. They have not grown.

They don't go to Bible study. They don't go to prayer meetings. They don't attend revivals. They never fast and they do not pray. Therefore, they are making the same mistakes and getting into trouble because they still don't know any better.

Guess what. I have another story for you. One day, a Sunday school teacher asked her class, "If you could be any Biblical character that you wanted, who would you chose to be, and why?" One little boy raised his hand and said, "I would be Moses because he was able to see God's glory." Another little boy raised his hand and said, "I would be David because he was the apple of God's eye." A little girl raised her hand and said, "I would be Mary because she was the mother of Jesus."

Little Johnny, who was sitting in the back of the class, raised his hand and said, "I want to be Low." The teacher said, "Johnny, there is no such person in the Bible", but Johnny was insistent. He said, "Yes there is, teacher. There is a person in the Bible whose name is Low, and that is who I would want to be."

The teacher said, "OK Johnny. Where in the Bible is there a person named Low?" Johnny said, "He is in Matthew, the 28th chapter, where Jesus said, "And Low, I am with you always." Then he said, "The rest of the class can be whoever they want, but I want to be Low, because I want Jesus to be with me always."

Although Little Johnny was confused in thinking that there was a person named Low, I agree with him. I want Jesus to be with me always too. When I am sick, I want Jesus to be with me. When I am in trouble, I want Jesus to be with me. When friends turn their backs on me, I want Jesus to be with me. When my family forsakes me, I want Jesus to be with me. Weeping may endure for a night but joy will come in the morning light. So hold on. Help is on the way. Hold on. Help is on the way.

Go ye therefore, and teach all nations, baptizing them in the name of the Father, and of the Son and of the Holy Ghost: Teaching them to observe all things whatsoever I have commanded you: and, **lo,** (surely) I am with you always, even unto the end of the world. Amen. (Matt.28:19-20)

CHAPTER SEVENTEEN

Shattered Dreams

It was the day before Thanksgiving in 1975. I was on a small-chartered plane that was flying over Amarillo, Texas. The pilot had just announced that we were going to make an emergency landing. I can remember thinking to myself, "I don't want to die like this. Not here. Not now. Then again, what difference does it make if my life is over with anyway".

You see, the plane that I was on was headed to the Federal Penitentiary at Leavenworth. As I sat there, chained and shackled to eight other prisoners, my mind began to wonder. What happened? How did I mess my life up so badly? What happened to all of the hopes and dreams that I had once had? I began thinking that it might be better if the plane did crash, and shatter into a thousand pieces, just like my dreams had. *Shattered Dreams.*

I was at the lowest point of my life. I was a high school drop out with a drug problem and a bad conduct discharge from the Marines. Now, I was sitting on a plane headed to one of the most notorious prisons in this country on the day before Thanksgiving. I thought to myself, "What do I have to be thankful for?" *Shattered Dreams.*

Oh yes, just like everyone else, I had dreams, but now, all I could do was just sit there, almost in a state of shock, wondering how I had gotten to this point. What had I done to deserve a seat on this plane?

I was not a hardened criminal, and I wasn't a bad person. I had grown up in a nice Christian home with a mother and father who loved me. My father was even providing for my college education while I was still in grammar school. So why was I sitting on a plane, on my way to prison with a federal record, instead of sitting on a plane, on my way home with a college degree. *Shattered Dreams.*

After we made the emergency landing in Amarillo, we sat on the plane for several hours while the mechanics made the necessary repairs. While we were sitting there, my mind went back to the Rose of Sharon Missionary Baptist Church in Chicago. I could see myself sitting there on the front pew with my grandmother and listening to Rev. Murphy.

I could see myself standing in the Baptismal pool at age nine, staring into Rev. Murphy's face as he was about to baptize me, and thinking to myself that one day I was going to be like him. I must have been dreaming because I could just feel the pride that I had as I stood at my post as a junior usher.

I could even remember the feeling I had years later, when at age 17, I stood in the pulpit of the Galatians Missionary Baptist Church and preached my trial sermon about Daniel in the lion's den. I was so desperately hoping that this was not a dream, because there I was, a teenager again, fellowshipping and hanging out with all of my Christian friends.

My life had meaning again. I felt like I could dream again. Dream of being a doctor. Dream of being a lawyer, an engineer, or anything I wanted to be, until I felt a sharp pain in my right knee. When I opened my eyes, I saw one of the prison guards standing over me holding a nightstick in his hand and telling me to fasten my seat belt. We were about to take off again.

When I looked around I quickly realized that I was not a teenager again. I was not in Church and these were not my Christian friends. I could forget about the dreams I had about becoming a doctor, or a lawyer, or anything else for that matter. It had all been just a dream. Now the plane had been repaired and I was on my way to Leavenworth Federal Penitentiary where I would have to trade my dreams in for a uniform with the numbers 59698. Shattered Dreams.

I want to ask you something. Do you have a dream? What is your destination in life? What are your goals? What are your objectives? Do you have a dream?

In the 37th chapter of Genesis, we see that Joseph had a dream, and he went through slavery and prison, but even with all that, he still knew that he was going to be somebody. Some of you have gone through some difficult situations as well. Maybe it was in your home. Maybe it was at your school. Maybe it was on the block while you were hanging with some of your partners. Maybe you've been experimenting with some things that you know you had no business messing with. Or you've been doing some things that you know is wrong. Now you are confused because your life is in shambles and you don't know what to do.

Well I want to tell you something. Your life is not over with. I don't care what anybody tells you, you can still be somebody. So don't let anything stop you from dreaming and don't let anyone discourage you from perusing your dreams.

If there was ever someone who should have been discouraged from dreaming, it was Joseph. Let us take just a minute or two and look at a portion of his story. Some people probably thought Joseph had no business dreaming in the first place. You see, in Israel, it was the firstborn son who was loved in a special way by his parents and he inherited special rights and privileges.

His Birthright was a double portion of the estate and the leadership of the family, but Joseph was not the first-born. As a matter of fact, he was the 11th of twelve sons. So what right did he have to dream? What made him think that he could possibly be somebody?

Some people feel that you don't have a right to dream either. They think you are just wasting your time dreaming of being a politician, an entrepreneur, or CEO of some major corporation. Your skin is the wrong color, your parents don't belong to the right club, or you were born on the wrong side of the tracks.

Oh yeah, they will try to keep you from dreaming, but I dare you to dream anyway. Dream as big as you can, and then place your dreams in the hands of God and watch what happens.

There was another group of people who thought Joseph had no business dreaming. They were his brothers. In fact, they hated him because he had dreams, but you don't have to take my word for it. Just look at the last part of verse 8. It says, "And they hated him all the more because of his dream and what he had said." He had told them that he was going to be somebody. Now, you would think that if anyone were going to be on your side, and want to see you succeed, it would be your family or those closest to you. Am I right?

However, there are some people who don't want anything out of life, and they don't want to see you with anything either. They are satisfied right where they are. Sometimes those are the ones that are closest to you, your friends, your family members or your classmates. They cannot see any further than where they are right now. They look at their surroundings and they believe that the only way that they can make it is by running with a gang, selling drugs, or ripping off their own people. They think that going to jail is a badge of honor. They have no hope. They have no vision. They have no dreams.

I once read that when a flea trainer is training his fleas, he places them in a jar. When he first puts them in there, they jump out because fleas are incredible jumpers. I mean, they can jump so high, that sometimes it looks like they can fly.

The training begins when he puts a lid on the jar. The fleas continue to jump, but when they do, they hit their heads on the lid over, and over, and over again. So after a while, the fleas continue to jump, but they no longer jump as high as they can, because they don't want to bump their heads anymore.

Now the trainer can remove the lid from the jar, and when he does, the fleas will continue to jump, but they will not jump out of the jar. Actually, they won't jump out because they no longer can jump out because they have conditioned themselves to jump just so high. Now, that is all they can do.

Some of you have conditioned yourselves to jump just so high because every time you have tried to jump any higher than that you have bumped your heads. You have bumped your heads on racism. You have bumped your heads on peer pressure. You have bumped your heads on people telling you what you could not do and what you could not be. You have bumped your heads over, and over, and over again because Satan had placed a lid over your dreams.

Well I want to serve notice on you. When Jesus died on the cross one Friday, Satan thought he had shattered His dreams too. But early that Sunday morning, when He stepped out of the grave, not only was the stone removed from the entrance to the tomb, but the lid was removed from above your dreams. That is why the Apostle Paul was able to say, *"I can do all things, through Christ who strengthens me."* *(Phil 4:13)*

So don't be afraid to aim high. Aim as high as you can. One of my former Pastors, Rev. Joseph Jones, used to say, "While you are aiming, aim for the stars, and if you fall upon the moon you will still be on higher ground." So aim high.

Joseph was not afraid to aim high, but there will always be someone who is jealous of what they may see in you and they will stop at nothing to try to destroy you and your dreams. Just look at verses 19 and 20 says, *"And they said one to another, 'Here comes that dreamer. Come now, let's kill him, and throw him into some pit, and we will say, some evil beast has devoured him. Then we will see what will become of his dreams."*

I want to let you in on a little secret. Sometimes you have to stop watching your enemies so close and start watching your back when your friends come around. Some of them are the real player haters. There are so many people whose dreams have been shattered by their friends.

I don't know of anyone who got their first cigarette or their first joint from one of their enemies. You never see a man standing on the corner drinking whiskey or wine with one of his enemies. It is not a person's enemy who talks them into smoking crack. It is not a person's enemy who gets them to cut class. It is not a girl's enemy that gets her pregnant. It is not a boy's enemy who convinces him to join a gang. It is not a person's enemy that can destroy his or her dreams in such a way, because no one would let their enemies get that close to them.

Only a friend, a very close friend, someone that you love and trust can get close enough to you to destroy your dreams in such a manner. So what are you saying, preacher? I'm simply saying that sometimes you have to take a step back and take a real hard look at the people that you call your friends.

My father tried to tell me that. He said, "Son. That crowd you're hanging out with don't mean you any good." I wouldn't listen. I said, "Dad. You don't know what you're talking about. These are my friends." I found out that he was right, because when I was in Cook County Jail, there were so many times that I sat there wondering, "Where are my friends now?"

When the guards were passing out the mail and they would walk pass my cell because I did not have any, I wondered, "Where are my friends now?"

On visiting days, I wanted somebody to come and see me, but I just sat there, trying to pretend that I wasn't hurting when my number wasn't called because no one cared enough to come. Many times, I just sat there in my cell, fighting back the tears, and wondering, "Where are my friends now?"

Sometimes I would think about all of the money I had thrown away on drugs, alcohol and wild parties trying to buy somebody's friendship. Now I couldn't even afford to buy a bar of soap to wash my face. I wondered, "Where are my friends now?"

In verse 27, we read that Joseph's brothers decided not to kill him, but to sell him into slavery. They decided to compromise. That way, they could destroy his dreams without taking his life. We see in verse 28 that they sold him to the Ishmaelites and he was taken to Egypt.

Let me ask you something. Are you on your way to Egypt? Have you allowed your dreams to be compromised and now you have found yourself in slavery to some drug that's ruining your life? Are you on your way to Egypt? Have you let someone convince you that you will never be anybody, or amount to anything? Are you on your way to Egypt? Do you think that it's OK to disobey your parents? Is it OK to lie, to cheat, and to steal, just because everybody else is doing it? Are you on your way to Egypt?

The last point that I want to make is that Joseph was not afraid to say no. In chapter 39, we see that Joseph had been sold to

Potiphar, who was one of Pharaoh's officials and the captain of the guard.

The Bible says that the Lord was with Joseph and he prospered, and he lived in the house of his Egyptian master. In the New International Version, Verse 7 says *"and after a while, his master's wife took notice of Joseph and said, 'come to bed with Me.' but he refused."* Joseph said, No. He knew what was at stake here. It was his relationship with God.

Oh yeah, Joseph was a dreamer, but he knew who gave him the ability to dream. It was God, and as long as he had a relationship with God, he knew that he could still dream, no matter what his situation or circumstances were. He knew that he had to make a choice. Either say no to Potiphar's wife, or say no to God, and to his dreams.

You have to make some choices too, and decide who you are going to say no to. Will it be to the temptations in life, or are you are you going to say no to God, and to your dreams? When your friends come to you trying to get you to do something that you know is wrong, who are you going to say no to?

Young ladies, when your "boo" comes to you, talking about, "If you love me you will go to bed with me." Who are you going to say no to? Young brothers, when your dogs come to you with that joint or that blunt, who are you going to say no to? When they come with that "Player's Pack" telling you how much money you can make selling dope and poisoning your own people, who are you going to say no to?

There are more than 2 million people who are in prison in the United States today. What happened to their dreams? Our streets are full of women and men who are addicted to crack and are selling their bodies for a ten dollar rock. What happened to their dreams?

So I want to ask you again, do you have a dream? What is your destination in life? Where do you want to be 10 or 20 years from now? Do you have a dream?

When the Dream Busters come at you, trying to make you lose your focus, what are you going to do? When things get so hard that you just can't see how you can make it, what are you going to do? Are you going to just give up and give in, or are you going to stand your ground and echo the words of the Apostle Paul? "I can do all things through Christ who strengthens me."

You guessed it. It's story time. Two fowlers went to a mountain to spread their nets so they could capture as many doves as possible. After they had set their traps, they left. When they returned, their nets were filled with doves. Desperately the birds flew back and forth trying to escape through the holes is the finely woven net.

At first the hunters were ecstatic over the large number of birds they had caught, but after examining them more closely, they were not very happy with their catch. You see, the birds were very small, and the fowlers were afraid that there would be no market for such skinny birds.

After thinking about it for a while, the men came up with a plan. They decided to buy some mash to feed the birds with, thinking that in a few weeks they would be nice and plump. Everyday the two men brought food and water, which the birds quickly devoured. Slowly, they began to grow in size, but there was one dove that refused to eat.

The other birds had gotten so comfortable in their situation, that they ate everything that the fowlers had brought them. They figured that since they were never going to get out of that net anyway, they might as well make the best of it. So they just laid around, eating and drinking, and getting bigger, and bigger.

However, that one obstinate bird was determined to make it. He refused to get comfortable. He refused to eat their food and he refused to quit struggling.

Then on the day the hunters came back to take all of the birds to market, the dove who refused to eat had become so skinny, that with one last mighty struggle, he was able to squeeze through the net and fly away. He was the only one that made it.

Are you going to be the one who makes it? Are you determined that you are going to do whatever it takes to achieve your dreams? Have you made up in your mind that you can do all things through Christ who strengthens you?

Oh yeah, Joseph achieved his dream. No matter how difficult his situation had gotten, he never gave up, and he always trusted in God. So no matter how rough the road may become, never lose sight of your dreams.

Always give it your very best, because one day you are going to stand before the Almighty God of the universe and He is going to ask you, "What did you do with the dreams I gave you?" What will your answer be? Are you going to say, "Lord, they wouldn't let me---? They wouldn't let me do anything. They wouldn't let me be anybody." Or will you be able to say, "Lord, I took advantage of every opportunity that you placed before me, and I did my very best to achieve every dream that you gave me."

So no matter what it is that you are called upon to do, do it with a spirit of excellence. My father used to say, "If a task is once begun, never leave it until it is done. Be the labor great or small, do it well or not at all."

So if you're called upon to build buildings, build the best buildings that have ever been built. If you are called upon to design clothing, design cloths so well that even kings and queens will be wearing your labels.

In the words of one the greatest dreamers of all time, Dr. Martin Luther King Jr., "If you are called upon to sweep streets, sweep streets like Michelangelo painted pictures. Sweep streets like Beethoven composed music. Sweep streets like Shakespeare wrote plays. Sweep streets so well, that all of the hosts of Heaven and of earth will pause and say, 'There goes a great street sweeper, who swept his job well'."

Dream on.

CHAPTER EIGHTEEN

I've Fallen, and I Can't Get Up

When I was nine years old, I sat in the back of the Rose of Sharon Missionary Baptist Church in Chicago and listened as my first pastor, the Reverend James A. Murphy preached a sermon about Adam and Eve. It was the first time I had ever heard the story so I sat there somewhat spellbound as he talked about the fall of man and the consequences that we all had to suffer because of the fall.

Although Ralph and I were in church every Sunday, I think that that was the first time one of Rev. Murphy's sermons really hit home with me. I loved to hear him preach Sunday after Sunday. It was through him that I first heard the story of the three Hebrew boys in the fiery furnace. I loved the one about Daniel in the lion's den.

There were so many sermons that he preached that made me feel good. The Prodigal Son, The Good Samaritan, and Lazarus being raised from the dead were just a few. I guess you can call those shouting sermons, but the fall of man was not a shouting sermon to me. The only thing that my little nine-year old mind could digest was that because of Adam's disobedience, I was going to have to die someday, and there was nothing that I could do about it. So in a sense, when Adam fell, I too had fallen, and I couldn't get up.

Naw, the story of Adam and Eve was not a shouting sermon, but in the case of the three Hebrew Boys, when Nebuchadnezzar looked in the furnace, and saw Shadrack, Meshack and Abednigo walking around in the middle of the fire with the Son of God, it was time to shout. When Daniel was thrown into the lion's den and God sent an angel to shut the lions' mouths, it was shouting time. When the Prodigal Son came walking down that dusty road and his father went running to meet him, it was shouting time, and when Jesus went to the graveyard and said, "Lazarus. Come forth", I tell you it was shouting time. Those are shouting sermons.

On the other hand, what about Adam and Eve? Let us examine their situation for a minute and see if we can find a place to shout. First, they let Satan fool them. Then, they disobeyed God. After that, they made excuses as to why they sinned. Then, among other things, they are kicked out of paradise and condemned to die. Where was the happy ending? Why would somebody want to shout after hearing that story?

I'll tell you, when I heard that sermon I was the most depressed nine-year old boy you ever wanted to see. I didn't even want to go outside and play after church, but I wasn't going to just take this laying down. I wanted to see what Paul had to say about this thing. In Romans 5:12, he wrote that "By one man (Adam), sin entered into the world, and death by sin: and so death passed upon all men, for all have sinned."

Now it sounds to me like Paul was saying that because of Adam, I was born into sin, and my man David didn't make things any better. He corroborated Paul's testimony in the 51st Psalm when he said, "I was born in sin and shaped in iniquity." In other words, I had inherited Adam's sinful nature.

Now do you see why I was so depressed? I was a good boy. I didn't drink. I didn't smoke. I didn't curse. I didn't run around in gangs. I went to church every Sunday and I was even on the Usher Board. I was a good boy. My parents and teachers bragged about how good I was.

David, Paul and Rev. Murphy were telling me that no matter how good I thought I was, I was still a sinner. I didn't want to be a sinner. I didn't even know what a sinner was. I was just nine years old.

You see, when Adam disobeyed God, he fell into sin, and all of mankind fell right with him. There are so many people who don't realize that they too have fallen. There are many people who are lost in sin who think just like I did. They think that they are going to Heaven because they are not that bad.

They don't get drunk, they don't do drugs, they don't steal, they don't cheat on their spouses, they give to charity, they don't gamble that much, they don't cheat on their taxes, etc. Many times those are the hardest ones to witness to because they think they are already good enough.

First, you have to realize that you are a sinner. You have to realize that you have fallen. You have to realize that you are lying in the gutter of sin and you have to realize that you cannot get up on your own.

When I was seven years old, I was playing in front of my house when a girl that was riding a bicycle ran over me and knocked me down. I kept trying to get up, but I couldn't. I was in a lot of pain. I didn't know that my leg was broken in two places. I remembered that my father was in the house and he had the window open so he could hear me if I called him. So I started yelling, "Daddy, Daddy." Before I knew it, he had reached down and picked me up.

There are many people who have been crippled by sin and they're lying there trying to get up all by themselves. Some people don't want any help from anybody. Not even God. You know the type. They are the ones who will stick out their chests and brag about being, "a self made man."

They are the ones who always want to get themselves together before they go to church. They'll say, "I've got to leave this alcohol alone first", or, "I've got to leave these drugs or alone first." "As soon as I get myself together then I'll go to church." Somebody who is reading this book is going through something. You know that you need the Lord but you want to get yourself together first.

God told me to tell you something. Stop trying to do His job. You can't get yourself together. That's like a sick person saying, "As soon as I get myself well, then I'll go to the hospital." You can't get yourself together. Only God can do that. As long as you keep trying to do it yourself, you're going to be like I was, trying to get up with a broken leg.

Someone's whole world seems to be coming apart. There is trouble in your home, trouble in your dorm, trouble with your family, trouble everywhere, and you just don't know what to do.

You have to remember that your Father is in the house and he has left the window open for you. All you have to do is just call on Him. You can't be too ashamed to call him. You can't be too proud to call Him. It's not too late. You're not too young or too old to call Him. If you just call Him, He will hear you, and He will reach down and pick you up.

There is something else that I want to tell you. Christians sometimes fall too. Oh yes we do. We may not want to admit, but we do.

There are many reasons that a Christian might fall from grace. Pride, peer pressure, and a prayer-less life are just a few. There is one reason that just confuses me to no end. That is success. How can success cause a Christian to turn their back on God?

Bishop T. D. Jakes once said, "When we are put into a place of prominence, many of God's children forget who brought them to that place. When Christians who are not rooted and grounded in the Word start acquiring prestige and experiencing monetary prosperity, in other words, they get a little money, they often forget that not long ago they had nothing.

Before they owned a nice new car, they could barely afford to ride the bus. Before they lived in a nice new home, their family of five lived a two-bedroom apartment not knowing how they were going to pay the rent. They were living from paycheck to paycheck, but in spite of it all, they still managed to give God the glory. They knew that God would meet their needs, but once they came to a place of prosperity, they forgot that it was God and God alone who blessed them. Now they look to their jobs or their businesses as their source, and that is a dangerous place to be because you're just setting yourself up for a fall."

I wish some of you could go with me to the jails and prisons and hear the men and women there tell of how they grew up in the church and how they wish they had never left. I told you about how I let people talk me out of the church, telling me to get out into the real world and see what life was all about. Six years later, I found myself on a plane headed to Leavenworth Federal Penitentiary. I'm not saying that everyone who leaves God, will end up in prison, but I am saying that you will end up some place that you don't want to be.

To fall is bad enough, but to fall and not cry out for help, refusing to repent of your sin, is worse than the fall itself. Maybe you are ashamed to let anyone know that you have fallen because you don't want them to think less of you.

I want to let you in on a little secret. Christians are not perfect. We are just forgiven. *"If we confess our sins, He is faithful and just to forgive us our sins and cleanse us from all unrighteousness." (1st John 1:9)*

So if you're not perfect, just remember, you're in good company. Let me mention just a few other people who were not perfect either.

Noah got drunk – after the flood. Abraham lied and said that Sarah was his sister – this was after God had called him out of Haran, and you know what they say, like father, like son. Isaac lied to Abimelech and the men of Gebar and said that Rebekah was his sister, and this was after God had told him how he was going to bless him.

God told Moses to speak to the Rock, but Moses disobeyed God and hit the Rock – and this was after the Mt. Sinai experience. David committed adultery – after God had made him king. Solomon worshipped idols – after God made him wise. Peter denied Jesus – after walking with the Lord for three years.

I'm not giving you an excuse to sin, but what I'm saying is, as great as these men were, Satan didn't leave them alone after God had called them. So what makes you think that he will leave you alone just because you have accepted Christ.

Now I realize that I no longer have to be depressed about the fall of man. Aw, I can shout about it now, because Jesus took a sad story and gave it a happy ending. *"As by one man's disobedience (Adam), many were made sinner, so by the obedience of one (Jesus), shall many be made righteous." (Romans 5:19)*

When Adam fell into sin, I had fallen too, but although I can't get up, I don't have to just lay there and wallow in my sins. I can call on Jesus and He will pick me up.

So, if Satan has knocked you down and you are going through something (You may have fallen back into your old habits or you may have picked up some new ones, and you just can't handle it, and you don't know what to do), just remember, your Father is in the house and He has left the window open. So if you call him, he will hear you. Just say, "Father, I need you Lord. Help me. I've fallen, and I can't get up."

My father told me a story about a little boy who was trying to move a huge rock that was in his back yard one day. His father stood there watching his son struggle with the rock. Finally, the father asked, "Are you using all of your strength, son?" The little boy said that he was.

The father watched his son a little while longer, and then he asked again, "Are you sure you are using all of your strength?" Once again, the boy replied that he was. After watching his son struggle unsuccessfully for a few more minutes, the father said, "Son, I know that you are not using all of your strength, because you haven't asked me to help you."

There are so many things that we struggle with in our lives, but we must realize that God is our strength and He just waiting for us to ask Him to help us.

David said, "The Lord is my strength."

Are you using all of you strength. When life knocks you down, are you using all of your strength? When temptation comes knocking, are you using all of your strength, or are you trying to do it all by yourself.

Just remember, your Father is in Heaven and he has left the window open. He is just waiting for you to call Him. All you have to say is, "Father, I've fallen, and I can't get up."

CHAPTER NINETEEN

I Ain't Gonna Do It No More

When I was very young, I don't remember exactly what age, a very popular song was played on the radio quite often. A group called The Coasters recorded it and the name of the song was "Charlie Brown". This is not the same Charlie Brown that appears in the Peanut cartoons and comic strips. There is quite a difference in the two. This Charlie Brown had a reputation of always goofing off in school and disrupting the class. In the song, they talk about some of the things that he does.

For instance, he walks in the classroom cool and slow. He calls the English teacher "Daddy-O." He's always running in the halls, writing on the walls and throwing spitballs.

What I used to admire most about Charlie Brown was his ability to get away with the stuff that he was doing. I know he got away with it because the song said, "he's gonna get caught", meaning he had not been caught, yet.

That might be the reason that I thought I could get away with something one Friday evening. Oh yeah, I remember that day very well. My father was at one of his union meetings, and my mother had walked down the street to visit one of her friends. Therefore, Ralph and I were home alone.

There was a different version of the song Charlie Brown that was going around at school. In that version, the words had been changed and there was a lot of cursing going on. Since we were home alone, Ralph and I decided to sing the school version of the song, curse words and all.

We were having a good time. The more we sang, the more we cursed. The more we cursed, the more we laughed. The more we laughed, the louder we sang. We were having a real good time until I noticed that Ralph had stopped singing. When I looked at him to see why he had stopped, I saw the look of shear terror on his face, and he was shaking like a leaf on a tree. I thought the boy had seen the "Boogey Man" or something.

When I turned to see just what had scared him so badly, I saw that it was not the "Boogey Man." It was worse. It was my mother standing there looking at us. She said, "Don't stop now. Keep on singing."

There were no child abuse laws back then. So she lit into my behind with that ironing cord. I kept yelling, "I ain't gonna do it no more. I ain't gonna do it no more", but she said, "I don't want to hear, I ain't gonna do it no more. I want to hear Charlie Brown. Sing Charlie Brown." No matter how hard I tried to sing Charlie Brown, the only words that would come out were, "I ain't gonna do it no more."

I knew what I had done was wrong, but at the time, it didn't seem to be that big of a deal to me. It was just a few bad words. It wasn't as if I had stolen something. So, although my cries of "I ain't gonna do it no more", were a form repentance, it was not true repentance because I was not truly sorry. I just wanted the punishment to stop.

That is how many people are. They are not truly sorry for the sins that they have committed against God. They just want Him to get them out of the mess that they are in. That's all. So they go to church and they sing their little songs, and they pray their little prayers, and they follow along in their Bibles. They say, "Lord, if you will just get me out of this mess, I promise I ain't gonna do it no more. I ain't gonna drink no more. I ain't gonna get high no more. I ain't gonna cheat no more."

There are a lot of people that knowingly and continuously step outside of the Will of God, and they think that it's not that big of a deal. They say, "I don't drink that much", or "I only gamble every once in a while", or "Everybody else is doing it." It's not like real sin.

Then they find themselves in the middle of a crisis and they cannot find their way out. There is trouble in their home. There is trouble on their job. There is trouble at their school. They get to the point where they just can't take it anymore so they fall down on their knees and cry out to God.

That is only a form of repentance. That is not true repentance because they are not truly sorry. They just want God to take away the pain and they want the suffering to stop.

Paul said, *Godly sorrow worketh repentance to salvation. (2 Cor. 7:10)* You have to be truly sorry. Ralph and I were not truly sorry for what we had done. If we were, we would not have done what we did next. Don't get me wrong. We did not sing Charlie Brown again. In fact, whenever they played Charlie Brown on the radio we changed the station. We didn't ever want our mother to hear that song again. Never.

I still don't listen to Charlie Brown today. My mother passed away in 2004, and I still change the station when that song comes on.

That is what we, as Christians, have to learn to do sometimes. We have to change the station. If your friends are causing you to sin against God, change the station. Stay away from those friends. If the places that you go bring on temptation, change the station. Don't go to those places. You might be holding on to some things that are not necessarily sinful or wrong, but every once in a while, they may cause you to stumble. You know what you have to do. You have to change the station. Get rid of it. Jesus said, "If your right hand offends you, cut it off."

Danny Thomas told a story about a man who walked into his doctor's office one day. He raised his hand high above his head and said, "Doc, it hurts when I do this." The doctor looked at him and said, "Then, don't do that."

All I'm trying to say is, if you are doing something that is hurting your relationship with God; you don't have to seek advice from anyone. You know what to do. Don't do that. Change the station.

Godly sorrow worketh repentance. To repent means to change, but some of us don't want to change completely because there are some things that we are just not ready to give up yet. So what do we do? We look for ways to get away with it. Then we say, "Nobody's perfect."

After my mother had whipped us for singing that night, she told us something that I have never forgotten. She told us to always watch what we say or do because, "Every goodnight is not asleep, and every goodbye is not gone."

Ralph and I thought about what she had said for a long time. At least until our behinds stopped hurting. Then we came up with some ideas on how to have our fun and get away with it.

My mother had said, "Every goodnight is not asleep." So if we were talking about something that we didn't want our parents to hear, we made sure that we were nowhere near their bedroom. She also had said, "Every goodbye is not gone." So before we did anything that we weren't supposed to be doing, we checked the hallway to make sure she wasn't coming up the stairs, we looked out the window to make sure that she wasn't coming down the street and we checked the back door to make sure she wasn't coming up the back stairs. Once we were satisfied that the coast was clear, it was party time.

Our mother had taught us a valuable lesson in those words that she had said, but we took those words of wisdom and used them to get away with our disobedience.

My friend, there are too many times that we read or hear God's Holy word, and then we twist it or use it to get away with sins that we don't want to stop committing. Do you have Godly sorrow for the sins that you have committed or are you looking for excuses to get away with them? When you repent, do you really mean it, or are you just saying, "Lord, I ain't gonna do it no more?

When I realized just how much I was hurting my parents with the things that I was doing I became truly sorry. When I saw the pain that I was causing them with my actions, I became truly sorry. When I realized how much they loved me, I became truly sorry.

Do you know how much you are hurting God with the things that you do? Do you realize just how much pain you are causing Him with your disobedience? Do you have any idea how much Jesus loves you? He has already died for you. So what would it take for you stop hurting Him? What will it take for you to be truly sorry?

This is the story of Charlie Brown after he had gotten older and quit school. We'll call it "Charlie Brown, The Sequel."

One day Charlie Brown decided to go fishing. He rented a small boat and went down to the lake. While he was out there, he started drinking. After awhile, he was so drunk that he fell overboard and was drowning. Just as he was going down for the last time, he felt a hand grab him and pull him to safety, saving his life.

Afterwards, the man who had rescued him sat him down and talked to him. He said, "Son, you need to change your lifestyle or you are going to get into some serious trouble one day." But Charlie just said, "Don't worry; I'm not gonna do it any more."

Not long after that, Charlie was home getting high and watching TV. After a while, he lit a cigarette and went to bed. He fell asleep while the cigarette was still burning and the house caught on fire.

While he was in the hospital, he found out that the man who had pulled him from the burning building and had given him CPR was the same man who had pulled him from the lake awhile back. Although the circumstances were different, his message to Charlie was still the same, "If you don't change the way you living, you are going to end up in some very serious trouble one day." Once again, all Charlie Brown said was, "Don't worry, I ain't gonna do it no more."

Then one Friday evening after Charlie had cashed his paycheck he decided to go shoot craps. He lost all of his money and didn't even have bus fare home, so he had to walk. The shortest way home was through one of the gang neighborhoods, so that was the way he went. Some gang members saw him and started chasing him.

While he was running, a car pulled up. Charlie recognized the driver. It was the same man who had saved his life twice before, so Charlie jumped into the car and they sped away.

The man turned to Charlie and said, "Young man, you've been given chance after chance. If you don't listen to somebody and change the way you are living, you are going to end up someplace where you really don't want to be." Once again, Charlie said, "Don't worry, I ain't gonna do it no more."

However, a short time later, Charlie got into a fight over some drugs and he killed a man. He was taken to jail and charged with murder. When he went to court, he was very nervous, but when the judge walked in, his face lit up. The judge was the same man who had pulled him from the lake. He was the same man who had dragged him out of the burning building. He was the same man who had rescued him from the gang bangers. Yes, the judge was his friend.

When Charlie Brown stood before the judge he said, "Hello your honor. I know that I have messed up a lot and I would not listen to you or any one else, but if you just give one more chance, I promise, I ain't gonna do it no more."

The judge looked at him and said, "I'm sorry, Charlie. It's too late now. When I came to you those other times, I was your savior. Today, I am your judge. Then he said, "Charlie Brown, I hereby sentence you to death."

My friend, today, Jesus is your Savior. He is saying to you, "Let not your heart be troubled. If you believe in God, believe also in me." Today, Jesus is your Savior. He is saying to you, "Come unto me, all ye that labor and I will give you rest." Today, Jesus is your Savior. He is saying to you, "Who so ever shall call upon the name of the Lord, shall be saved." I'm telling you, Jesus is your Savior today. I know He is your Savior because I hear Him saying, "This day, if you hear my voice, harden not your heart."

I beg you, come to Jesus while you have time. Don't be like Charlie Brown and just keep saying, "I ain't gonna do it no more," and continue living your life as usual, or one day you will not be standing before a loving Savior. You will not be standing before a faithful friend. You will be standing before judgment.

"I saw a great white throne and Him who sat on it. And I saw the dead, small and great standing before God, and the books were opened. And another book was opened which is the book of life. And the dead were judged by the things that were written in the books. And anyone who was not found in the book of life was cast into the lake of fire. (Revelation 20:11-15)

My friend, right now, Jesus is your Savior, but one day He will be your judge. There was an old song that my grandmamma used to sing. It said:

There's no hiding place down here
There's no hiding place down here
I went to the rock - to hide my face
The rock cried out- there's no hiding place
There's no hiding place down here

I've got good news for you. There was another song that I heard her sing.

Amazing grace
How sweet the sound
That saved a wretch like me
I once was lost
But now I'm found
Was blind but now I see

Through many dangers
Toils and snares
I have already come
Twas grace
That brought me safe thus far
And grace will lead me home

CHAPTER TWENTY

Chump Change

In many of my sermons, lectures and speeches, I talk about some of people that I grew up with, or who were an important part of my life in one way or another. Over the years, I have talked about Fuzzy, Gip, Tadpole, and even my dog, Rex.

The other day, as I was thinking about some of my old friends, and there was one person in particular that crossed my mind. His name was Chucky. You might remember me mentioning him in my first book. Chucky was a little older than I was and a lot bigger. Since he had been through a lot and was a friend of the family, he tried to keep me out of gangs and out of trouble. For a long time he had been somewhat successful.

I remember something else about Chucky. He was cheap. When we were teenagers, we would all get together on Friday nights and put our monies together to buy some beer or wine. All of us would chip in our dollars, but when it came to Chucky, all he would ever come up with was a quarter, or maybe fifty cents. We would get mad and start getting on his case and telling him to come up with some more money, but all he would ever say was, "Sorry y'all, but all I've got is some chump change."

We knew that Chucky had some money. After all, he received an allowance just like the rest of us, but whenever we were putting our money together to buy anything, no matter what it was, all Chucky would ever come up with was some chump change.

For those of you who may not know what chump change is, it is money that you don't really need. It is money that you can afford to throw away. It is what you give to the men and women that are standing on the street corners begging for spare change so they can get something to eat. It is what the crippled man that is in the fifth chapter of Acts was asking Peter and John for. In other words, it is what many of us give to God every Sunday morning. Chump Change.

Oh yeah, we give God our leftovers. We furnish our beautiful homes, drive our expensive cars, and wear our designer clothes with our finest jewelry. We buy the best of everything for our children and even make sure that our pets are well taken care of. We go to the malls and "shop til we drop", and then we go to church on Sunday morning and give God our chump change.

Cheating God does not always start when we become adults. Satan starts working on us while we are children. I remember when I was about 10 years old. Ralph and I used to walk to the church down the street from our house, Rose of Sharon. My father gave each of us a quarter to put in the offering. However, there was one thing that was wrong with that plan. Between our house and the church house, there was a candy store, Jenkins Grocery. For some reason, we just could not get past Miss Jenkins' store with our quarters. By the time we got to church, all we had left was a nickel and a pocket full of candy. In other words, all we had left to give to the Lord was some chump change.

It is not only with our finances that we shortchange God. We sometimes give Him chump change in other areas of our lives as well. Our time. Our talents. Our worship, and our praise. I'm convinced that we don't do better, simply because we don't realize what a mighty God we serve. I know I'm right about it because if you knew how good God really is, you would not be satisfied with being where you are. You might be asking, "Where am I then, preacher?" I'm glad you asked.

In the above-mentioned text, Peter and John were on their way into the temple to pray. Outside of the temple, there was a gate. Seated at the gate was a man that was crippled. The Bible says that his friends would carry him to the gate everyday so he could beg from the people who were on their way into the temple.

Now, I don't believe that this man was the only one who used to sit at that gate. I don't believe he was the only one because, whenever someone comes up with a way to get something for nothing, no matter how legitimate the need, there is always going to be somebody else that is trying to do the same thing. Am I right?

Therefore, that is probably where most of the crippled folks hung out. They were outside of the church, sitting at the gate, begging for chump change. That is where some of you are right now. You are at the gate with all of the crippled folks because you too have been crippled.

Some of you have been crippled by heartaches. You've been crippled by disappointments. You have been crippled by family problems, crippled by failed relationships or crippled by your financial situation. Sometimes you feel like giving up because you have been crippled by circumstances that are beyond your control. You are overwhelmed and you don't know what to do.

What you don't realize is that, no matter how big your problems seem to be, to God, they are just chump change. Instead of taking your problems to the Lord, you started hanging out at the gate with all of the other crippled folks and feeling sorry for yourself.

The Bible says that the man was satisfied just sitting at the gate, outside of the church, every-day, begging for chump change. Too many Christians have gone outside of the church looking for what they think is the answer to their problems. They have gone to the gambling boat looking for the answer. They have gone to the liquor store looking for the answer. They are standing in the lottery line looking for the answer.

The Bible says that when Peter and John were about to enter into the temple, the man asked them for some money. When he did that, the Bible says that they looked straight at him. Yes, Peter and John looked straight at the man. Now, why is that important? Why did Luke feel it was important that we know that the apostles looked straight at the man?

Well, I believe it was important because too many of us, when we see someone who needs help, we turn our heads and look the other way. You know that I'm telling the truth.

There are certain kinds of people that we just don't want to look at. We don't want to look at that drunk who is standing on the corner. We don't want to look at that prostitute who is jumping in and out of cars. We don't want to look at that drug addict who is standing there, nodding and scratching. We don't want to look at that homeless person that is begging for some chump change. We don't want to look at them because it makes us uncomfortable.

Nevertheless, Peter and John didn't turn their heads and keep on walking. The Book says that they looked straight at the man. If you think that was something, look at what happened next. Peter said, "Look at us." First, the disciples made sure that they looked at the man. Now they want the man to look at them.

You notice Peter didn't say, "Look at me." He said, "Look at us." I think Peter said "Look at us" because he remembered what Jesus had told them one day when He said, "Where two or three are gathered together in my name, there I am in the mist of them." So when Peter said, "Look at us," he was not telling the man to look at him and John. He was telling him to look at Jesus.

The Bible says that the man gave them his attention because he was expecting to get something from them, but he didn't get what he was expecting. He was expecting to get what he had always gotten.

He was expecting to get a hand out. He was expecting to get some chump change.

Instead, Peter said, "Silver and gold have I none, but what I do have I give unto you. In the name of Jesus Christ of Nazareth rise up and walk."

Peter didn't just tell the man to get up. The Bible says that he took him by the hand and he helped him up. You need to hear that because our communities are full of people who are lost and hurting. Many of them are at the point where they feel helpless and hopeless. Satan has put them on his hit list. Drugs are pulling at them. The streets are pulling at them. Some of them were even members of a church at one time. Now they're sitting at the gate, begging for chump change.

We have to do what Peter did. First, we have to get their attention. And when we get their attention, when they are looking at us, we have got to make sure that they see the love of Jesus in us. Then, we can't start preaching at them and telling then they ought to get up. We have to reach down, take them by their hands, and help them up. Sometimes you can't share your faith with them, until you show some faith in them.

The Bible says that after the man was healed, he got up and went into the temple. When he went in, he went in walking, and jumping, and praising God.

There are so many people that God has been good to, but for one reason or another, they won't give Him any praise. They don't even get to church on time because they don't want to be there for praise and worship. The only time they will clap their hands is when the music gets good. They want the choir to sing them happy or the pastor to preach them happy.

I remember my partying days, and if I was going to a nightclub, I didn't wait until I got there to get into the partying mood. I didn't depend on the music or the other people to set the tone for me. While I was on my way to the club, or sometimes before I had even left home, I was getting into the partying mood. I had already started drinking and getting full of the other "spirits."

While I was getting dressed, I had The Temptations playing on the stereo, and I was getting in the partying mood. While I was on my way to the club, I was anticipating how much fun I was going to have once I got there. When I got to the club, I walked in singing. I walked in dancing. I walked in having a good time, because I had prepared myself for the party before I had even left home.

Wouldn't it be something if on Sunday mornings we would start preparing ourselves for worship before we left home? Wouldn't it be something if when we got out of bed, we asked God to fill us with His spirit, and while we were getting dressed, we were praising Him and worshiping Him? While we were on our way to church we were praising Him and worshiping Him, and when we got to church we walked in the door, just singing and dancing, and praising the Lord. Oh, what a time we would have in the Lord.

Satan was about to lecture some of his young recruits on the fine art of deception. "Before I begin," he said, "I would like to hear what you consider to be the best methods of leading people away from God."

The first recruit said, "I think the best method is to convince people that there is no God." "Not good," said Satan. "We call that, 'The Frontal Attack.' It has been used for centuries, but without great success because only a handful of people ever accept true atheism."

The second recruit said, "Maybe we could convince people that there is no hell." Satan sighed and said, "That was very successful for a long time, but we have promoted so much hatred and war that now people sense that they have to account for the evil they do."

Another recruit suggested that they plant the idea that God is so easy-going that there is no need in making an immediate decision. "Tell them they have plenty of time," he said.

"Ah, You have stumbled on our second best method of deception." said Satan. "Procrastination! For centuries, it has been our best method with the youth. Its only defect is that it is ineffective with some of the older people."

"Then what is the best method of deception," the recruits all asked.

Satan said, "Our best method works with those who go to church regularly as well as those who do not. It works on the old and the young, the rich and the poor, the blacks and the whites. It even works on some of the members of the church.

We call it 'Moderation.' We convince people that it is all right to go to church, but they don't have to go every Sunday. Just go in moderation.

We tell them it's all right to read a few verses in the Bible and say a prayer occasionally, but don't do it every day. Do it in moderation.

We make them believe it is all right to give a small offering, but don't tithe or give anything extra. Give in moderation.

We convince people not to get too excited or fanatical about God. We convince them that all He really requires of them is a little chump change. This way they convince themselves they are Christians. However, in truth, there is no fire in their souls. Yes, moderation works just about every time."

CHAPTER TWENTY ONE

I Ain't Got To Live Like This

In chapter one, I talked a little about Freddy's barbershop and some of the players that frequented his establishment. Now I want to tell you the rest of the story.

Freddy's was not your typical barbershop. There were no signs outside to advertise it, and all of the windows were painted black, so no one could see inside. Therefore, most people didn't even know that it was a barbershop, or a business establishment at all, for that matter.

Not just anyone could go into Freddy's. The door was always locked, and if Freddy didn't know you, or you were not with someone that he did know, he would not let you in.

That was where all of the players and hustlers went to get their hair done.

After I was released from Leavenworth Federal Penitentiary, I started smuggling drugs out of California and delivering them to the Chicago area. During one of my trips, I decided to rip off the people that I was doing business with. I was going keep all of the money and all of the drugs. So I came to the conclusion that it might be in my best interest not to go back to California.

I stayed in Chicago and did my hustling there. I started hanging out with some of the other players that were in the area. Players like Red, C.J., Pretty Tony, and Slick Rick. Since all of the other players were wearing perms at that time, I decided to get my hair done too. So one Saturday evening, C.J. and Red took me to Freddy's Barbershop.

The thing that I liked best about Freddy's was the party atmosphere. Since Freddy was the only hairdresser, there were always a few people sitting around and waiting. However, there was always a lot of drugs and liquor there too, so nobody really cared about the wait.

The other thing I liked about Freddy's was it was kind of a school for hustlers. There were always one or two pimps or players there that had been in the game for a while, and they would be bragging about their accomplishments and sharing their knowledge of the fine art of hustling with the rest of the patrons.

I remember one Saturday in particular. It was during the summer of 1976. One of the well-known and highly respected pimps was getting his hair done. While he was in the chair, he was sharing his philosophy of life with the rest of us, and because of his reputation and his notoriety, we were all hanging on his every word.

He said, "You know, there are two kinds of people in this world, the players and the squares." He said, "The squares have to get up and go to work everyday for some chump change because that's the only way they can make any money. They don't know how to play the game. They're too busy living their dull, boring lives and trying to stay out of trouble, but us players, we know the game. We drive the baddest rides, we got the prettiest women, we've got all the money, and we do whatever we want to do, whenever we want to do it." Then he said, "I don't know about y'all, but as long as I live, I'm gonna be a player."

That was the attitude I had, and the way I lived my life for the next 11 years. Then I went back to prison. There is one incident in particular that stands out in my mind to this day. It was in the early part of 1987. I was in the state prison in Joliet, Ill. for parole violation. I remember sitting on that cold, hard concrete floor, chained and shackled to about 20 or 30 other men while we were waiting to be taken across the street to general population.

What I remember most about that day was a voice I heard from the other side of the room. I couldn't see who was talking because there were too many people in between us. Even though his voice sounded somewhat familiar, it was what he said that sounded even more familiar.

He said, "You know, there are two kinds of people in this world, the players and the squares." He said, "The squares are at home with their families right now. They are eating what they want to eat, going where they want to go, and doing what they want to do, whenever they want to do it. But us players, we are sitting here, on this cold, hard floor, all chained up like a bunch of animals. We got somebody telling us where to go, what to do, what to eat, when to eat, and when to sleep " Then he said, "I don't know about y'all, but whenever I get out of here, I'm gonna be a square, cause I ain't got to live like this"

As I stated earlier, our disobedience and rebelliousness puts us in difficult situations. The Bible is full of stories of people who were called or chosen by God, but for one reason or another they strayed away from Him and everything they had ever been taught. Our jails and prisons are full of them too.

I didn't realize this until I was teaching a Bible study class at one of the jails in St. Louis about 12 years ago, and one of the inmates had to step out of the room. As he was leaving, he held up that "Baptist finger." When I saw that, I asked, "How many of y'all grew up in church?" You would be surprised at how many of them raised their hands.

That was a shock to me, but it shouldn't have been, because I too, had grown up in the church, and look where I had been. I spent 22 years of my life, in and out of jails and prisons because of a drug and alcohol problem.

Jesus told the story that is found in Luke 15: 11-32 about a young man who left home in order to live a lifestyle that was contrary to the way he was brought up.

Verses 11-13 says, *"A certain man had two sons: And the younger of them said unto his father, 'Father, give me the portion of goods that falleth to me.' And he divided unto them his living. Not long after that, the younger son got together all he had, set off for a distant country and there squandered his wealth in wild living."*

What happened to this young man? How did he stray so far away from his father's teachings? The Bible doesn't tell us how much time had elapsed between the time he left home and the time he had completely lost his way, but I don't believe it happened over night. I don't believe his downward spiral began after he had left home. I believe he strayed away the same way that sheep stray away from their shepherd. He nibbled himself away.

I don't claim to know a lot about sheep. We didn't have a lot of them in Chicago, at least not in my neighborhood, but I am told they are not very smart. A herd of them might be walking along, following their shepherd and the rest the sheep, but at the same time, some of them will be nibbling at the grass. They will nibble a little and then look up to make sure they are still following the shepherd and the sheep.

Sometimes there is that one sheep, or that one lamb, that gets so engrossed or so caught up in his nibbling that he forgets to look up. He's just wandering along with his head down, enjoying the grass so much that he just nibbles, and nibbles, and nibbles. When he finally does look up, he doesn't see his Shepard anywhere, and he doesn't see the rest of the sheep. He is lost. He has wondered off in the wrong direction, and he cannot find his way back. He didn't mean to get lost. He just nibbled himself away from the fold.

Our jails and prisons are full of men and women who have nibbled themselves away from the God. They've nibbled themselves away from the church. They've nibbled themselves away from everything had ever been taught. They are not bad people. They were just nibbling.

Some of them were doing O.K. until they got curious and they started nibbling on marijuana. Some of them were doing all right until they started hanging out with the wrong crowd, and they started nibbling with the gangs. Some of them had even gone off to college, and things were going great until they started nibbling on alcohol. Some of them had good jobs and they were respectable citizens until the started nibbling on crack. They just nibbled, and nibbled, and nibbled until one day they looked up and they were lost.

People start nibbling at different stages of their life. Some start when they are young, others start when they are older. Unfortunately, some of them start nibbling while they are still in church.

That was what I did. I started nibbling when I started hanging out with some of the guys that I worked with. Sometimes they would get together and drink beer after work, and eventually I started drinking with them.

They were always asking me to go to the club with them after work. Finally, one Friday I went with them. I still remember that night. We were in the car on our way to a club called "The Bird Cage" located on the south side of Chicago, when one of them lit a joint. I had never smoked marijuana before, but I didn't want them to know I wasn't as cool as they thought I was, so when they passed me the joint, I took it.

I found myself going to church less and less. I started hanging out with Fuzzy, Chucky, and Butch again. Eventually, I stopped going to church at all. I just got drunk, smoked weed, and partied all the time. I was going from one drug to another: Reds, acid, trees and finally heroin, cocaine, and then crack.

Just like that lost sheep, I had my head down and I was nibbling, and nibbling, and nibbling. By the time I looked up, I had nibbled myself out of the church and into a drug habit, and then, into prison.

Verses 14-16 say, *"After he had spent everything, there was a mighty famine in that whole country, and he began to be in need. So he went and hired himself out to a citizen of that country, who sent him into the fields to feed pigs. He longed to fill his stomach with the pods that the pigs were eating, but no man gave him anything"*

Do you know how it feels to be without hope? No hope of ever becoming anything? No hope of ever being truly happy? Just going through life without any hope at all? I don't believe that when this young man left his father's house, he could have ever imagined that he would end up in a pigpen. Likewise, when I left the church, I never imagined that I would end up on drugs and in prison.

I never thought the day would come when I would be lost and without hope. There were so many times that I asked myself, "How did I mess my life up so badly?" There were times that my mind would go back to the Rose of Sharon Missionary Baptist Church, when I was nine years old and sitting on the front pew with my grandmother and ushering with my Aunt Ruth. I thought about how happy I was when I stood in the pulpit of the Galatians Missionary Baptist Church and preached my trial sermon.

What I remember most was sitting in my car outside of a drug house in K-Town one night, waiting for Tadpole to come out with the heroin. I was sitting there, listening to the radio and watching the building that he had gone into. I was watching the surrounding area, looking out for the police and the stick-up man.

Although I wasn't listening to a Christian station, a church song came on the radio. I just happened to look in the side mirror, and what I saw completely messed me up. I saw the St. James Church of God in Christ, where I had preached one of my last sermons about twenty years earlier.

I just sat there, listening to that church song and looking at that church building where I had had so much fun praising the Lord and being with my Christian friends. I found myself crying and reminiscing and wishing I had never left the church, but it was too late. I had messed up too badly. I had nibbled myself completely away from God and into a world of hopelessness. I hated my life. I hated myself. I hated what I had become. I hated the drugs, the jails, and the drunkenness, but what I hated most of all, was the hopelessness I felt.

I thank God for verse 17. It says, *"When he came to himself, he said 'How many of my father's hired servants have food enough to spare, and here I am starving to death. I will arise and go to my father and say unto him, Father, I have sinned against Heaven and against you.'"* In other words, what he said was, "I ain't got to live like this. I'm getting up from here. I'm going back home where I belong, cause I ain't got to live like this." He got up out of that pigpen and he headed home.

When I was in the Cook County Jail, Rev. Jerry Hodges would come there every Sunday, trying to talk the inmates into going to the church services. I never would go. I thought I had done too much wrong for God to ever forgive me. Besides, I didn't want to appear to be weak to the other inmates.

However, one Sunday evening, I decided to go ahead and go to church. While Rev. Hodges was preaching, he said, "I bet a lot of y'all wonder why you are in this jail." He said, "You are here because, when you were running the streets, doing your thing, God couldn't get your attention. So He allowed you to be put someplace to slow you down so He can get your attention and you can hear Him. He does that because He loves you." Then he said, "No matter what you have done. No matter what you have become, God still loves you."

That was the day that I realized that I didn't have to live that lifestyle any longer. That was the day that I realized that I no longer had to be lost and without hope. That was the day that I understood what that old pimp had meant years earlier, when we were all chained up, and he said, "I ain't got to live like this." My life was changed that day, forever.

That is why I do prison ministry. So many men and women are in jails and prisons all across this country who are tired of the way they have been living. They are tired of drinking. They are tired of drugging. They are tired of prostituting. They're tired of jailing. They are getting up out of the pigpens of derogation and despair, and saying, "I ain't got to live like this," and they are turning their lives over to the Lord.

This country prides itself in being called the land of the free, but too many of our men and our women are anything but free. They are still in slavery. They are in slavery to drugs. They are in slavery to the gangs. They are in slavery to black-on black crime. They are in slavery to an unfair justice system. Yes, they are in slavery.

Just before Jesus told the story of the lost son, He told another story. It was the story of the lost sheep. I want to tell you that story, but I'm not going to tell it the way that Jesus did. This is **NOT** in the Bible, so don't go looking for it in there. In order to get my point across, I want to use my spiritual imagination and tell it a different way. Is that all right?

When Moses was forced to flee from Egypt, he went to the land of Midian where he found a job, tending sheep for a man named Jethro. Moses was a good Shepherd. He spent his days tending and caring for his flock. He knew each sheep and each lamb, and he could call them by name. Moses remembered his people who were living in bondage, and were being oppressed by the cruel Egyptian slave drivers. He longed for the day when God would free them and lead them back to their own country.

One day, Moses led his flock of 100 sheep across the desert to the foot of Mt. Sinai. When it grew dark, he started counting the sheep before leading them home, but he discovered that one of them was missing. Looking around, he found tiny hoof prints leading toward the mountains. The little lamb had nibbled himself into dangerous territory.

What should he do? Should he lead the 99 back to Jethro's home or should he leave them there and search for that one lost lamb? Although it was a tough decision, he could not bear the thought of abandoning that tiny lamb. So leaving the 99, Moses raced up the side of the mountain, following the hoof prints as best he could. All night long, he searched, looking behind every bush and behind every rock.

Finally, towards morning, he found the trembling lamb, weak and frightened. He lifted it unto his shoulders rejoicing, and headed back down the mountain.

Suddenly he saw an eerie sight. A bush was on fire, but the flame did not consume it. Then he heard a voice that came from the bush. "**Moses, Moses**." "Here I am," he said. "Do not come near." said the voice. "Take off your shoes, for the place where you are standing is holy ground.

"Moses, I am the God of Abraham, the God of Isaac, and the God of Jacob. Just as you have saved this stray lamb, I have chosen you to save my people from slavery in Egypt."

All this time, Moses was still holding the stray lamb on his shoulders. Then he realized that he was being called to carry Israel on his shoulders out of slavery.

I want to ask you something. What is God calling you to do? Drugs have taken over our communities. People who were once considered respectable citizens are selling their bodies and committing crimes to support their habits. The prison industry is the fastest growing business in our nation.

You might be the one that God is going to use to stop this madness. You might be the one that God is going to use to bring His people out of slavery. You might be the one that God is going to use to bring His people back to Him, but you won't be any good to anyone if you start nibbling.

For too long the church has been hiding behind its sanctified walls and singing, "I am on the battlefield for my Lord" and then going home after the benediction and saying, "Somebody ought to do something about those people." I want to serve notice on you. You are that somebody.

I know that you have faith in God and in the saving power of Jesus Christ. Now I challenge you to share your faith with the outcast of this society, and let them know that Jesus loves them.

One Sunday evening, God looked down on a street hustling, dope shooting, jailbird like me. Because of His grace, and mercy, He saved my soul.

Amazing grace
will always be my song of praise.
For it was grace
that brought my liberty

I do not know
just how He came to love me so
He looked beyond
my faults and saw my needs.

I shall forever
lift mine eyes to Calvary
To view the cross
where Jesus died for me

How marvelous
the grace that caught my falling soul
He looked beyond
my faults and saw my needs.

CHAPTER TWENTY TWO

THAT'S MY STORY,
AND I'M STICKING TO IT

In 1984, a young man by the name of Larry Johnson was accused of a crime that he did not commit. Although he had proclaimed his innocence to everyone who would listen, from the Justices of the Supreme Court all the way down to his cellmates, he was still found guilty and spent the next 18 years of his life in prison.

For 18 years, day in and day out, the authorities, other prisoners, and probably even some of his own attorneys tried to convince him to admit his guilt. They told him that if he would just "fess up and show a little remorse," he would probably get out of prison a lot sooner.

For 18 years, day in and day out, he stood firm. He said, "I don't care if nobody believes me. God is my witness. I've told you what happened. Now that's my story, and I'm sticking to it." After 18 years, they found out that he had been telling the truth all along.

Let me ask you something. Do you have a story? Is there something that you feel so strongly about that no matter what the consequences are you are unwilling to waiver? Do you have a story? Has your life been changed so drastically that your friends, family members, or co-workers can no longer understand you? They cannot understand why you don't curse anymore. They can't understand why you don't get high with them anymore. They can't understand why you want to go to church, read your Bible and pray so much now. They just can't understand what has happened to you. Do you have a story? The woman at the well had a story. (John 4: 5-30) While she was drawing water one day, Jesus stopped by. After spending just a few minutes with the master, the Bible says that she got so excited, that she left the water and the jar at the well, ran back to town, and told everybody to "Come, see a man". She had a story to tell.

The man with Leprosy had a story. (Mark 1: 40-45) He was a social outcast because of his disease. He came to Jesus on his knees one day, begging Him to make him clean. After Jesus had healed him, He told the man not to tell anyone. After thinking about it, I think this is the same man that wrote that song that my Grandmamma used to sing. "I said I wasn't gonna tell nobody, but I couldn't keep it to myself." He just couldn't keep news like that to himself, because the

Bible says that he told everybody what the Lord had done for him. I'm telling you, after he met Jesus that day; he had a story to tell.

The Apostle Paul had a story. (Acts 9:1-16) You remember Paul don't you? He was one of the religious leaders of his time. However, Paul had one problem. He didn't know Jesus, but there is nothing strange about that. There are some religious leaders today that don't know Jesus. There are some preachers that are sitting in the pulpit that don't know Jesus. There are some church members that are singing in the choir that don't know Jesus. There are some deacons that are sitting on the front pew that don't know Jesus. There are some church members whose names are on the roll, and have been there for years, but they don't know Jesus. There are some chaplains that are working in the prisons that don't know Jesus. Paul didn't know who Jesus was. One day, Paul (Saul) and his friends had just left his church's state convention and were headed to Damascus when Jesus showed up. He knocked Paul off his high horse and introduced Himself. You know, the Lord has to do that to us sometimes. In order to get your attention, He has to knock you off your high horse.

After Paul met Jesus that day, the Bible says that when he got to Damascus, and the Lord opened his eyes, he found himself on Straight Street. That is what the Lord will do for you. He will open your eyes and then take you off of Drunk Drive and put you on Straight Street. He will take you off Crack Court, and put you on Straight Street. He will take you off Liar's Lane, and put you on Straight Street. He will take you off My Way Highway, and put you on Straight Street. He will take you off Sin Sick Blvd., and put you on Straight Street.

When Paul left Straight Street, the Bible says that every time he got a chance, he told his story. He told it to King Agrippa one day. *Agrippa said, "Paul, you've almost persuaded me to be a Christian." (Acts 26:28)* He told it to Festus one day. (Acts 26:24) Festus said, "Paul, I think you have gone crazy. There just ain't no way that I'm going to believe what you are telling me", but Paul said, "I'm not crazy. I'm just telling you, what the Lord has done for me. Now, that's my story, and I'm sticking to it."

The blind man had a story. (John 9:1-34) He had been blind all of his life. In fact, he was born blind. He used to hang out down at the gate with all of the other blind folks until he met Jesus one day. Jesus touched him and opened his eyes. The Bible says that his friends and family didn't recognize him. They said, "Hey dog. Ain't that Bub over there? You know, the guy that used to get high with us down at the gate." Somebody else said, "Naw man, that ain't Bub. He just looks like Bub.

The man overheard them talking and he said, "Hey y'all, it is me." Then they said, "Hey, what happened to you? Why do you look so different now? And how come you don't hang out down at the gate any more?" The man said, "I'm glad you asked. Step over here and let me tell you about Jesus. Let me tell you what He has done for me, and what He can do for you too." Aw yeah, he had a story to tell.

The Bible says that they tried to get the man to change his story. Just like Larry Johnson, they wanted him to change his testimony. They wanted him to quit talking about Jesus and go back down to the gate. They even went to his parents, hoping that they could talk some sense into him. They said, "What's wrong with your son, Bub? All he does now is go to church and talk about Jesus. What's wrong with him Mrs. Barr?"

That's just how Satan is. If he can't get to you, he will try to work through somebody else to get to you. He will try to work through your parents or your friends. He will try to work through your brothers or sisters. He will try to work through your husband or your wife. He will try to work through your room mate or your celly. He will work through anybody that he can, trying to destroy your testimony. The Bible says that the man wasn't trying to hear none of that. He said, "You don't know like I know what the Lord has done for me. You weren't there. There may be a lot of things that I don't know, but there is one thing that I do know. I once was blind, but now I see. Now that's my story, and I'm sticking to it."

All of the people that I've talked about have three things in common. First of all, they all met Jesus one day, and when they met Him, they knew without any doubt that He was the Christ. I want to ask you something. Have you met Jesus? Do you know, that you know, that you know, that He is your Lord and Savior? If you do, then you should share the second thing that they have in common. They all had a story. They had a story about how they met Jesus and what He had done for them. Do you have a story? If someone were to ask you to tell him or her something that Jesus has done for you, what would you say? What is your story? What would tell some lost soul or some backslider who needs to hear about God's saving grace? What is your story?

I have a story. I told it in my first book, throughout this book, and in churches and prisons all over the country, but I don't mind telling it again. Jesus came into my life and saved my soul when I was nine years old. Eleven years later, at age twenty, I walked away from God, His church, and the ministry that He had called me to. During that time, I made some bad choices. Because of those decisions, I ended up on drugs and in prison. I felt alienated from God. I thought I had done too much wrong for God to ever forgive me. I truly thought that there was no hope for me.

One Sunday evening when I was at the Cook County Jail, I went down to the worship service. There was preacher there by the name of Jerry Hodges. He told me that no matter what I had done, or no matter what I had become, Jesus still loved me. After I got out of prison, I went back to my same old ways. However, my life would never be the same, because he had planted the seed that day. Early one Sunday morning I had just left the drug house with a bag of heroin and a bag of cocaine. I was walking past a church house and I heard the sermon that was being preached. It was the story of The Prodigal Son. The next thing I knew, I was sitting on the church steps, in the rain, with heroin and cocaine in my hand, crying like a baby, saying, "Lord, I'm sorry, Lord, I'm just so sorry. Please forgive me for the life I've been living. I'm so sorry." I am not saying that I have lived a perfect life since then. I haven't. I am not saying that I have not made any mistakes along the way. I have. What I am saying is, on that day, God changed my life forever. ***Now that's my story, and I'm sticking to it.***

The third thing that they had in common was they told their story to anyone and everyone who would listen. Who have you told your story to? Somebody needs to hear it. There are people who you come in contact with everyday that are lost and on their way to hell. They need to hear your story. Someone may be ready to end their life right now because they just can't deal with the hurt and pain any longer. They need to hear your story. Someone is going through a very serious illness. I'm telling you, somebody needs to hear your story. So tell your story. Last December I was diagnosed with prostate cancer. I had surgery in February. I am still going through the healing process. Although it is long and tedious, the Lord is bringing me through it.

Speaking of stories, I have one more that I want to tell you. A tribal chief would go to God on behalf of his people whenever there was a crisis. He would go to a special place in the forest, light a special fire, and say a special prayer, and God would come to their aid.

When his successor faced a crisis, he would go to that special place in the forest to pray. He would say, "Lord, I do not know how to say the special prayer, but here I am, at the special place, and I have lit the special fire. Please let that be sufficient." It was.

When he died and his successor faced a crisis, he would go to that special place in the forest to pray. He would say, "Lord, I don't know how to light the special fire, and I don't know how to say the special prayer, but here I am at the special place. Please let that be sufficient." It was. When he died, his successor became the intercessor. When there was a crisis, he would kneel at the foot of his bed and pray. He would say, "Lord, I don't know how to light the special fire, and I don't know how to say the special prayer. I can't even find the special place in the forest, but I can tell the story. Please let this be sufficient." It was. When God saved your soul, He gave you a story to tell. So tell the story. When you are on your job, tell the story. When you are at school, tell the story. When you are at the grocery store, tell the story. When you are at the commissary, tell the story. When you are at the barbershop or beauty shop, tell the story. Every time you get a chance, tell the story.

Tell the story of how Jesus was wounded for your transgressions, and He was bruised for your iniquities. Tell the story of how He hung from an old Roman cross from the sixth to the ninth hour. Tell the story of how the sun refused to shine, because two Sons couldn't shine at the same time. You ought to tell the story today.

Tell the story of how He was buried in a borrowed tomb, but don't let the story end there. Be sure to tell the rest of the story. Tell the story about that Sunday morning when He got up from the grave with all power in His hands.

Blessed assurance, Jesus is mine
Oh what a foretaste of glory divine
Heir of salvation, purchased of God
Born of His spirit, washed in His blood
Perfect submission, perfect delight
Visions of rapture, now burst on my sight
Angels descending, bring from above
Echoes of mercy, whispers of love
This is my story. This is my song
Praising my Savior all the day long
This is my story. This is my song
Praising my Savior all the day long

TELL THE STORY, AND STICK TO IT!

ABOUT THE AUTHOR

Rev. Burton Barr, Jr., Associate Minister
West Side Missionary Baptist Church

Rev. Burton Barr, Jr. has served as one of the associate ministers of the West Side Missionary Baptist Church under the leadership of the Rev. Dr. Ronald L. Bobo, Sr. since 1994. He is a member of the senior staff and serves as Director of the Prison, Substance Abuse, and Outreach Ministries.

He also serves as Director of Prison Ministry for the Missionary Baptist State Convention of Missouri, and the Berean Missionary Baptist District. He is Commissioner of Prison Ministry for the National Baptist Convention U.S.A., Inc., and Chairman of the St. Louis Clergy Coalition's Law and Order Committee. He is a member of the Coalition of Prison Evangelist (C.O.P.E.), the Eastern Missouri Coalition To Abolish The Death Penalty, and the Missionary Baptist Ministers Union of St. Louis & Vicinity.

Rev. Barr is the author of the best-selling autobiography, "The Hoodlum Preacher." He preaches and teaches the Gospel of Jesus Christ in jails and prisons all over the state of Missouri and in many parts of the country. He also preaches and lectures at churches, youth rallies, and youth revivals in an effort to keep our young people from ending up in the prison system. He has been certified by the Missionary Baptist State Convention of Missouri's "Congress of Christian Education" to teach prison ministry classes.

He is a native of Chicago, IL. and is currently a student at St. Louis Christian College majoring in Christian Ministry. He is the husband of Charlotte Anne Barr, and is a proud father and grandfather.

BOOKS BY BURTON BARR JR.

He's Only A Prayer Away
Book Coming Spring 2009

The Hoodlum Preacher:
I Was Lost, Now I Am Found
(Paperback)

The Hoodlum Preacher:
Film Tie-in Edition
(Paperback)

The Hoodlum Preacher:
Film Tie-in Edition
(Audio Book)

Amazing Grace:
The Storm Is Passing Over
(Audio Book)

Additional copies of this book and other titles
from **Kobalt Books** are
available at your local bookstore.

KOBALT BOOKS

For a complete list of our titles,
Visit us online at our website:
www.kobaltbooks.com

DEVOTION NOTES

DEVOTION NOTES

DEVOTION NOTES

DEVOTION NOTES

DEVOTION NOTES

DEVOTION NOTES

DEVOTION NOTES

DEVOTION NOTES

DEVOTION NOTES

DEVOTION NOTES

DEVOTION NOTES

DEVOTION NOTES

DEVOTION NOTES

DEVOTION NOTES

Printed in the United States
202722BV00002B/1-195/P

9 780976 911753